THE COMPLETE GUIDE TO THE MUSIC OF

DAVID B

D1263190

Edited by Chris Charlesworth
Cover & Book designed by 4i
Picture research by Nikki Russell

ISBN 0.7119.5301.5 Order No.OP47799

Exclusive Distributors
Book Sales Limited, 8/9 Frith Street, London W1V 5TZ, UK.
Music Sales Corporation, 257 Park Avenue South, New York, NY 10010, USA.
Music Sales Pty Limited, 120 Rothschild Avenue, Rosebery, NSW 2018, Australia.

To the Music Trade only
Music Sales Limited, 8/9 Frith Street, London W1V 5TZ, UK.

Photo credits
Cover pictures: LFI. All others supplied by Andre Csillag, LFI and Barry Plummer.

Every effort has been made to trace the copyright holders of the photographs in this book but one or two were unreachable. We would be grateful if the photographers concerned would contact us.

Printed in the United Kingdom by Ebenezer Baylis & Son, Worcester.

A catalogue record for this book is available from the British Library.

CONTENTS

INTRODUCTION

It's very hard to be indifferent about David Bowie. For over a decade, from his British breakthrough as Ziggy Stardust in 1972 to the mainstream pop of 'Let's Dance' in 1983, he was undoubtedly the coolest and most innovative British pop star around. He was an ever-moving target – glam rock one year, soul the next – wrong-footing his critics and constantly placing demands on his fans, who learnt very quickly that they must move with his flow or be left behind. Bowie's flighty musical nature has occasionally led to disappointment and failed expectations for fans and critics who haven't been able, or haven't wanted, to take the trip.

For some, Bowie died with Ziggy. For a good many he was effectively finished when he started courting the mainstream in the early Eighties. For others it was the Glass Spider tour, a demeaning piece of over-theatricality; or Tin Machine, a ghastly experiment in hard-rock chumminess. So, Bowie's famed changes in musical persona have been just as much a handicap as a help. He's won, lost and re-won his audience three times over.

In the Eighties and Nineties Bowie's past achievements were tarnished, partly by his inability to match his Seventies work with anything as interesting, and partly because of a sea-change in rock sensibilities. Bowie, an artist who has always mixed media and incorporated references from film, literature and art into his music, was seen as an over-preening dilettante in an age when the authentic rock of Clapton and Springsteen came back in vogue. He still has an army of detractors in the media who would have us all believe that popular music should never rise above its entertainment status and should be about honesty and purity. But those who like their pop to come with a dash of theatricality, pomposity and even deceit still value Bowie as their champion. You'll always be surprised by Bowie, and even if he falls flat on his face with his latest project he'll always be back the year after with another one.

And Bowie's music is only half the real story. His power as a pop icon comes as much from his visual presentations on video and on stage, and from the complex relationship with his fans, than it does from music alone. But what a wondrous musical legacy it is, including eight UK Number 1 albums (only three of them in the Seventies) and no less than twenty-three Top 10 UK hits to date. If you're coming to Bowie for the first time there's almost certain to be at least one era you'll enjoy, whether it be the androgynous glam-slam of Ziggy, the hip soulster from his 'plastic soul' phase, the icy European technocrat of his Eno triptych in the late Seventies, the svelte Eighties pop star or the increasingly arty experimentalist of the Nineties.And, unlike virtually all other major pop figures from the Sixties and Seventies, McCartney, Clapton, Jagger and Dylan *et al*, he hasn't fallen back on the comfy notion that a mid-life career in rock should consist of pandering to the public will by endlessly re-hashing past hits on boring stadium tours.Bowie waved bye-bye to his back catalogue of hits on the Sound + Vision tour in 1990 and shows little sign of basing future tours on songs he recorded half a lifetime ago. He is still looking to the future, still bringing the mainstream's attention to the mass of innovative work going on around its margins, and as long as he's still around, the future will always be worth listening to.

I have restricted my analysis to Bowie's currently available product (although this varies all the time, and from country to country) and have not included the many compilation albums released by RCA during the early Eighties without Bowie's active involvement. Completists will doubtless criticise me for leaving some Bowie stuff out but there's a lot to cram in. There has not been space, for example, to go into Bowie's career as a record producer or to detail all of his many guest appearances on a variety of recordings. The UK magazine *Record Collector* has published numerous detailed articles on Bowie's recording legacy for those with more particular interests. In this book I have decided to cover his most important recordings in some detail at the expense, necessarily, of some lesser material. All his studio and live albums, from 'Space Oddity' to 'Ziggy Stardust The Motion Picture' (excluding 'Peter And The Wolf'), were re-released in the early Nineties by Rykodisc in the USA and EMI in Britain. The packaging is often excellent, the sound quality has certainly improved and most of the albums contain bonus tracks which will obviously appeal to his hardcore fans but will naturally annoy purists to whom the extra five tracks on Ziggy Stardust after the final note of 'Rock'n'Roll Suicide' are simply an annoyance. There is still some RCA material which awaits baptism on CD, however, notably 1982's 'Baal' EP.

At the time of writing there are further re-issues, compilations and various live shows due to hit the racks in 1996 as well as a new Bowie album. Busy times ahead.

Over the years I've been lucky enough to receive encouragement and advice from a legion of friends and critics, all of them with something to say on the fortunes of Mr Bowie. I would like to thank in particular John Buckley, who didn't know what he was letting himself, or anybody else, in for when he played 'Hunky Dory' to me on Christmas Day 1973, and Ann Henrickson for commenting on my work and having to put up with Bowie in the house, and in my head, for so long. Thanks also to the many fans who have been so generous with their time: Dean Balaam, former editor of the now defunct fanzine *Zi Duang Provence* and Steve Pafford, editor of the really excellent Bowie magazine *Crankin' Out!*, P.O. Box 3268, London NW6 4NH, England. For info on *Crankin' Out!* please send Steve an SAE, or, if you're outside the UK, two IRCS. Getting hold of new Bowie material can be a problem. If it's rarities and imports you're after try Marshall Jarman, P.O.Box 18, Macclesfield, Cheshire, England. For an overview of Bowie's career, then Radio 1's *The David Bowie Story*, broadcast in six parts in 1993 and presented by Paul Gambaccini, is well worth listening out for in the event of a future repeat. And if this book hasn't sated your thirst for all things Bowie then there's Elizabeth Thomson and David Gutman's edited anthology of important essays and reviews, *The Bowie Companion* (Sidgwick and Jackson, 1995), or my own cultural biography of the man – *David Bowie: Strange Fascination* – to be published in 1996 by Liverpool University Press.

DAVID BUCKLEY, October 1995

All the material reviewed relates to the CD versions unless otherwise stated.
All songs are by David Bowie unless otherwise stated.

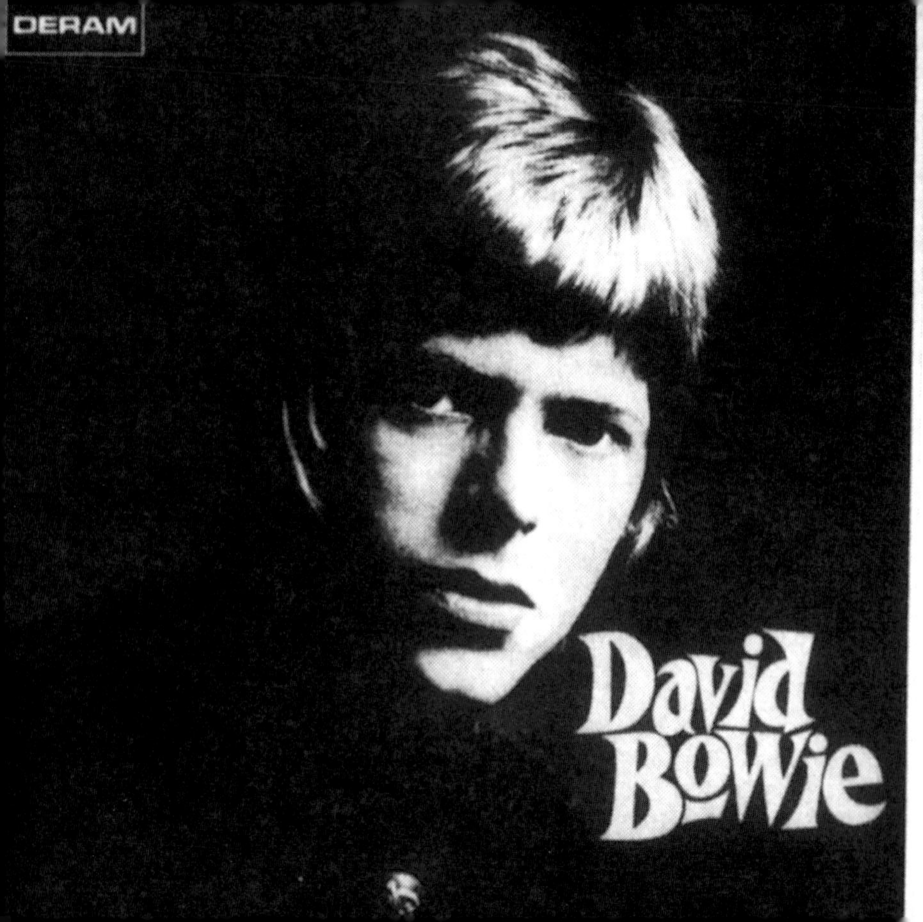
DERAM
David
Bowie

DAVID BOWIE

(ORIGINAL UK ISSUE: DERAM DML 1007, RELEASED 2 JUNE 1967; UK CD: DERAM 800 087 2; DID NOT CHART)

Bowie's eponymously-titled début album was released by the progressive label Deram at the high-water mark of Britain's counter-culture. It was not Bowie's first appearance on vinyl however. He had written songs and performed for a succession of short-lived beat and rhythm-and-blues outfits since 1964 (The Konrads, The King Bees, The Manish Boys and The Lower Third) as David/Davey Jones with little artistic or commercial success. There was, in truth, nothing in his mid-Sixties musical beginnings to suggest the innovative work to come. For those interested in Bowie's earliest work, see the compilations listed in the appendix at the end of the book.

His first album, produced by Mike Vernon, is as unlike the rest of the Bowie canon as one could imagine, consisting of fourteen short narrative vignettes delivered in a mannered music-hall cockney indebted to Anthony Newley. Manager Ken Pitt, who directed Bowie away from rock-and-roll and early on recognised his innate sense of theatre, encouraged the young Bowie's wildly eclectic tastes, and an unashamedly bizarre range of topics found their way on to the album. Gus Dudgeon, producer of Bowie's first hit 'Space Oddity' and later producer on many years of Elton John's platinum-selling albums, reminisces: "Listening to it now I can't believe that it was actually released because it must have been about the weirdest thing Deram had ever put out. In fact it must be about the weirdest thing any record company have ever put out."

And Dudgeon is absolutely right. The album has an English music-hall demeanour with the use of the waltz on 'Little Bombardier' and 'Maid Of Bond Street', and the overall impression is of a style of music located well outside the pop mainstream. The strings, bassoon and trumpet dove-tail with the dreaded neo-classicism heralded in by The Beatles on 'Sgt. Pepper' which was also released that year, but Bowie's use of classical music is grafted not on to rock or pop music but on to an odd pantomime ballad style. At best, though, his mini London Town dramas read like third-rate Ray Davies.

Bowie was, however, beginning to explore some of the themes he would later develop with far greater clarity on future albums. 'She's Got Medals' gives a foretaste of the cross-dressing themes of many of his early Seventies songs, and 'London Boys' deals with drug abuse and alienation (but without the sense of near glorification found on 'Aladdin Sane' or 'Diamond Dogs').

Perhaps the clearest indication of Bowie's future direction comes on 'Join The Gang' and 'Please Mr Gravedigger'. The first contains a jaundiced view of hippy culture: for Bowie, the idea of communality and shared love, which the counter-culture reputedly cherished, would prove anathema to his narcissism, sense of alienation and hard-headed commerciality. 'Please Mr Gravedigger' is arguably the most bizarre moment on any of his albums, with Bowie as a soliloquising child-murderer. The song itself comes on like a macabre parody of the bonhomie of a song such as 'Oh Mr Porter'. Delivered without instrumental backing, the lyrics are supplemented by a number of special effects (thunderclaps, raindrops, a bell tolling), creating a pop equivalent of a radio play. Bowie even fakes a sneeze or two, showing an early predilection for the sort of theatricality which would become his trademark.

Interestingly, 'David Bowie' was not included in the Rykodisc/EMI set of CD re-mastered re-issues in the early Nineties, as Bowie presumably wanted to keep this frequently cringe-inducing piece of juvenilia locked away in the vaults. However, it does exist on a Deram CD for all those with a high enough embarrassment threshold. Unfortunately, the downright stupid, though perversely endearing, 'The Laughing Gnome', a UK Top 10 hit in 1973 and a Seventies children's favourite (lovingly introduced on the *Tony Blackburn Show* as a song from Uncle David Bowie!), is nowhere to be found. Not even the *NME*'s 'Just Say Gnome' campaign, orchestrated to have the track included on the set list for the dial-a-hit Sound + Vision 1990 tour, could persuade Bowie of the need for a re-mastered version. An even more embarrassing track, 'Rupert The Riley', about a favourite motor-car and dating from around 1970, has cropped up on various bootlegs but also seems sadly destined to remain in the Bowie vault.

Full track listing: 'Uncle Arthur', 'Sell Me A Coat', 'Rubber Band' (Version 2), Love You Till Tuesday', 'There Is A Happy Land'. 'We Are Hungry Men', 'When I Live My Dream' (Version 1), 'Little Bombardier', 'Silly Boy Blue', 'Come And Buy My Toys', 'Join The Gang', 'She's Got Medals', 'Maid Of Bond Street', 'Please Mr Gravedigger' (Version 2).

DAVID BOWIE

(ORIGINAL UK ISSUE: PHILIPS SBL 7912, RELEASED 4 NOVEMBER 1969. RE-ISSUED ENTITLED 'SPACE ODDITY', RCA VICTOR LSP 4813, RELEASED NOVEMBER 1972; UK CD: EMI EMC 3571; US CD: RYKODISC RCD 10131) UK CHART: NO.17 [TOTAL WEEKS IN CHART: 38]; US CHART: 16 [10])

Bowie's second album was a vast improvement on his first, but is hardly an essential purchase for those coming to his music for the first time. The vocal is still reedy and uncomfortable on the ears and, 'Space Oddity' aside, there's nothing on the album to match his Seventies writing. That said, there are glimpses – 'Cygnet Committee' is a decorous folly with a stream of consciousness lyric assessing the counter-culture over a musical backdrop showing all the twists and turns of structure so beloved of progressive rock at the time. 'The Wild Eyed Boy From Freecloud' is a beautifully poetic song with an acute observational sensibility. Lyrically, however, the most important song is also the most direct – 'Janine'. When he sings 'But if you took an axe to me/You'd kill another man not me at all' the idea of Bowie at a distance from his real self (the theme which would dominate his work in the first half of the Seventies) comes across loud and clear. 'An Occasional Dream' and 'Letter to Hermione' show Bowie in weepy mood and concern his first real love, Hermione Farthingale, a member of Bowie's mime troop Feathers.

But it was 'Space Oddity' itself which rightly won all the plaudits. The album's producer Tony Visconti refused to have anything to do with it, seeing it as a cheap cash-in on the recent Apollo moon landing, and the session was produced by Gus Dudgeon. It's still a wonderful, if dated, epic of alienation, undoubtedly influenced by Stanley Kubrik's *2001: A Space Odyssey*, telling the tale of astronaut Major Tom, destined to roam the universe forever: 'planet earth is blue/and there's nothing I can do'. The entire song was also a metaphor for drug-taking, the countdown sequence intended to mirror the lag between an injection of heroin and the hit. It became Bowie's first big success, reaching Number 5 in the autumn of 1969 (it later reached Number 15 in the States and Number 1 in the UK in 1975), but it failed to break him into the big time as more flop singles soon followed. After an unsuccessful solo tour Bowie 'retired' to his multi-media Arts Lab in Beckenham and waited for the future.

What Bowie needed was a plan, and competition. The latter came from his friend Marc Bolan, whose career was about to take off with 'Ride A White Swan'. The strategy came from Bowie's decision to really dress up pop performance (undoubtedly aided by mime artist Lindsay Kemp whom Bowie had befriended), to play characters on stage in order to hide his real self from the sort of hostility he encountered on a recent tour. In February 1970 at the Round House, Bowie and his band The Hype performed in costume – Bowie as 'Rainbowman', Tony Visconti as 'Hypeman', Mick Ronson as 'Gangsterman' and drummer John Cambridge as 'Cowboyman'. The Hype bombed but Glam rock was born. The future of pop was altered irrevocably.

'Space Oddity' comes with three bonus tracks – the pleasingly whimsical 'Conversation Piece' and two very good versions of 'Memory Of A Free Festival' , the first Bowie music to feature the myriad talents of the late Mick Ronson.

Full track listing: 'Unwashed And Somewhat Slightly Dazed', 'Don't Sit Down', 'Letter To Hermione', 'Cygnet Committee', 'Janine', 'An Occasional Dream', 'Wild Eyed Boy From Freecloud', 'God Knows I'm Good', 'Memory Of A Free Festival'; bonus tracks on 1990 re-issue: 'Conversation Piece', 'Memory Of A Free Festival Part 1', 'Memory Of A Free Festival Part 2'.

David Bowie
The man who sold the world

THE MAN WHO SOLD THE WORLD

(ORIGINAL UK ISSUE: MERCURY 6338041, RELEASED APRIL 1971 (UK) NOVEMBER 1970 (US), RE-ISSUED: RCA VICTOR LSP 4816, RELEASED NOVEMBER 1972; UK CD: EMI EMC 3573; US CD: RYKODISC RCD 10132 UK CHART: 26 [TOTAL WEEKS IN CHART: 31] US CHART: 105)

This is the first of Bowie's truly essential albums. Its futuristic visions of a technologically mediated hell, snapshots of almost Bosch-like perversions, and fixation with madness and paranoia make this one of his most harrowing albums to date. It is also his most personal. In their book *Alias David Bowie* (Hodder & Stoughton, 1986), Peter and Leni Gillman unearthed a history of mental illness in the Jones family which has obviously had a direct influence on his writing. Forced to exorcise or transcend this legacy through dealing with it in fictionalised form, Bowie, on this album, in fact makes the plight of the mentally ill (particularly that of step-brother Terry, eight years his senior) more real.

'The Man Who Sold The World' was, up until the first 'Tin Machine' album, Bowie's most hard-rock oriented album. Although Mick Ronson's solos do dominate, the music, courtesy of the Moog synthesiser, also has a forbidding futuristic feel, harsh and unrelenting on 'Saviour Machine', macabre and child-like on the merry-go-round pop of 'After All'.

Recorded in late 1970, the successful realisation of the project owes much to the arranging skills of Mick Ronson and the production of Tony Visconti (who also played bass on the record). During this phase Bowie was at his most eclectic in terms of his range of interests (apparently developing a long-standing love of art during this period), and at his least disciplined when it came to the actual writing and recording (with only a handful of recording sessions actually attended by the man himself). This indiscipline was to lead to Visconti leaving the Bowie camp to concentrate on T. Rex's more formulaic, though initially more commercial, singles pop.

The re-issued CD now comes with the original cover art work featuring Bowie in his Gabriel Rossetti look with flowing locks and equally flowing knee-length skirt.

WIDTH OF A CIRCLE

Clocking in at over eight minutes, this is one of Bowie's most important early Seventies songs and is the album's pivotal track. A neat, infectious Ronson riff introduces a song which builds into a tale of Kafkaesque proportions. Bowie begins in picaresque mood before the killer couplet, 'then I ran across a monster who was sleeping by a tree/ And I looked and frowned 'cos the monster was me', re-introduces the central theme of split personalities. What then ensues is no less than an account of a homoerotic encounter with God in the Devil's lair, before a Ronson guitar solo and timpani roll draw this quite remarkable piece of music to a breathless halt.

ALL THE MADMEN

Descant recorders give this tale of madness a child-like intensity. The lyrics, a comment on Terry's own stay at the Cane Hill mental asylum, tell the tale of how the disturbed are interned in 'mansions cold and grey'. The track was successfully updated for the 1987 Glass Spider tour.

BLACK COUNTRY ROCK

The mood is temporarily lightened with this catchy piece of rock. In the early Seventies Bowie and Bolan, although sometime friends, emerged as media rivals, and this track is notable for Bowie's quite accurate Marc Bolan take-off towards the end.

AFTER ALL

Bowie was beginning to self-consciously target a following of blighted, disillusioned hippies, and this song speaks to them, melding the warped music-hall of his earlier work with a queasy fairground-ride melody. Although never a single, its use in Alan Yentob's 1975 BBC Omnibus documentary *Cracked Actor* as the background music to a camera sweep along a line of war-painted American Bowie fans, has provided an image as powerful as any video.

RUNNING GUN BLUES

This pop-rocker is truly bizarre. The lyric is a

puckish commentary (and deliberate trivialisation) on war-time atrocities in an era when pictures from Vietnam were flooding the media daily. Bowie's gung-ho, proto-Rambo figure is a product of diseased contemporary mores, and the throwaway nature of the song merely makes the effect more telling.

SAVIOUR MACHINE

From a contemporary and real dystopia to an imagined one. 'Saviour Machine' deals with a future society dominated by technology which has outstripped the human intellect. The bleakly insistent synth is this track's stand-out feature.

SHE SHOOK ME COLD

Groups such as Led Zeppelin and Black Sabbath were beginning to make what was later termed heavy metal *de rigueur*. It's easy to forget that this song arguably, if only fleetingly, puts Bowie (or perhaps more accurately Ronson) in the vanguard of the development of the style.

THE MAN WHO SOLD THE WORLD

With the album's finest melody, this continues the favourite theme of ego-stratification, as Bowie and *alter ego* meet on the stair. Nirvana's cover of the song on their 'Unplugged' album helped to re-acquaint the American public with Bowie's work after a low-profile period. The track was also successfully covered by Lulu in 1974, becoming a UK Top 3 hit with Bowie co-producing and providing backing vocals and sax. However, the best version was given by a mannequin-like Bowie himself late in 1979 on *Saturday Night Live*, with Blondie's Jimmy Destri on keyboards and Klaus Nomi on backing vocals.

THE SUPERMEN

Originally the album's closing track, this reveals Bowie with a head full of Nietzsche. Bowie was to draw on the idea of the superhuman potentialities of mankind later in 1971 when framing his omnipotent Ziggy Stardust character.

BONUS TRACKS ON 1990 RE-ISSUE:

LIGHTNING FRIGHTENING

This is a pleasant enough song and a not unwelcome bonus sweetener.

HOLY HOLY

Although the sleeve notes state that this is the 1971 single version, it is actually the Spiders-era re-make which became the B-side of the 'Diamond Dogs' single in 1974.

MOONAGE DAYDREAM & HANG ON TO YOURSELF

These two tracks (later re-worked and massively improved for the Ziggy Stardust album) were released as a single in 1971 under the name Arnold Corns, essentially a Bowie-centered project. In true Warholian style, clothes designer and friend Freddie Burretti was the band's front-person despite contributing almost nothing to the music save some vocals on another Bowie song, 'Man In The Middle'. This was not part of the Rykodisc re-issues but released with 'Looking For A Friend' and 'Hang On To Yourself' on vinyl in 1985 on the Krazy Kat label.

HUNKY DORY

(ORIGINAL UK ISSUE: RCA VICTOR SF8244, RELEASED 17 DECEMBER 1971; UK CD: EMI EMC 3572; US CD: RYKODISC C 10133; UK CHART: 3 [TOTAL WEEKS IN CHART: 122] US CHART: 93)

1971 was an enormously productive year for David Bowie. Now signed to a major label, RCA, and with manager Tony Defries and his Mainman company building up public expectations that Bowie was the next big thing, he wrote an enormous amount of material which would later be featured on both 'Hunky Dory' and 'Ziggy Stardust'. These two albums are, for many, still Bowie's finest-ever contribution, and remain essential purchases. He now also had in place the musicians who would soon become The Spiders From Mars, with Ronson and drummer Mick 'Woody' Woodmansey, retained from 'The Man Who Sold The World' sessions, joined by Trevor Bolder on bass guitar.

'Hunky Dory', recorded at Trident Studios in London and produced by Ken Scott (assisted by 'the actor', i.e. Mr Bowie), shows Bowie's music acquiring a whimsical melodic sheen after the hard rock of 'The Man Who Sold The World'. Hunky Dory is, in fact, one of his most conventional albums in purely musical terms – Rick Wakeman's piano and Ronson and Bowie's acoustic guitar dominate, with Ronson's string arrangements on 'Life On Mars?' and 'Changes' giving the music a stirring and dramatic edge. However, its easy-listening status has drawn attention away from the disturbing imagery found on songs such as 'Oh You Pretty Things!', and particularly the epic 'The Bewlay Brothers', undoubtedly one of Bowie's finest songs.

Released late in 1971, the album and lead-off single 'Changes' both flopped badly. It was not until its lofty successor had bitten hard into the nation's consciousness that the undoubted charms of 'Hunky Dory' were given their rightful status.

CHANGES

This song, more than any other in the Bowie canon, has an almost manifesto-like quality. For Bowie, whether we like it or not, it would always be (sing along now!) Ch-ch-ch-Changes. Vacillation was to become an organising principle. Bowie also neatly restates his position as poseur: 'Look out all you rock-and-rollers'. For him, if it had to be rock, it had to be rock done as an outsider, as a thespian, commenting on rock, never becoming a rocker in reality. It is a great tune too, and, amazingly, despite its appearance in almost every Bowie greatest hits compilation, never a hit single.

OH! YOU PRETTY THINGS

This song had already been covered by Peter Noone (ex-Herman's Hermits) and had reached Number 12 in the UK charts. The music here is almost 'McCartneyesque' but the lyric, dealing as it does with cracks in the sky and other manifestations of split personality, reveal a man still fit for the psychiatrist's couch.

EIGHT LINE POEM

A simple piano part and Ronson's light, country-style guitar is the backdrop for Bowie's parodic cod-Yankee drawl. It must come as no surprise that – unlike Rod, Elton or Mick – Bowie, since he was born in England, sang with a sarf-London accent as opposed to being Kentucky-Fried like most of his contemporaries. The theory went that if you sounded American you were closer to the blues masterprint and thus more 'authentic' and honest. Bowie, quite properly, thought all this was rubbish, thus helping to pave the way for the caterwauling cockney of Johnny Rotten five years down the line. No longer did Deptford have to sound like Dallas.

LIFE ON MARS?

With one of pop's most stirring melodies, this has gone on to become one of Bowie's best-loved songs, and was a Number 3 hit in the UK at the height of Ziggy-mania in July 1973. In fact, Bowie was conducting a little-known musical vendetta. He had been asked to write a set of lyrics to a French melody, 'Comme D'habitude', but they were rejected and Paul Anka was asked to submit a different set. The result was 'My Way', endless Sinatra comebacks and the Karaoke evening down the pub. 'Life On Mars?' is therefore a pretty neat parody of 'My Way', utilising a very similar four-bar melody. Bowie was not only settling an old musical score (no pun intended!) but was also signalling that he too could now be counted amongst the greats of popular music.

KOOKS

This is a fey, twee, but very popular, paean to his newborn son Zowie. 'Kooks' is all pretty strings and cod precautionary lyrics: 'Don't pick fights with the bullies or the cads/'Cos I'm not much cop at punching other people's Dads'. Not silly enough to be likeable and not camp enough to be kitsch, this is the album's only weak spot and is notable only for the fact that Morrissey plagiarised the line about throwing your homework on to the fire for the fab Smiths' song 'Sheila Take A Bow' a decade and a half later.

QUICKSAND

After the candyfloss of 'Kooks' the mood is immediately darkened with the arrival of this piece of philosophising about the futility of the human condition. A rag-bag of name-dropping and highbrow referencing (there's an allusion to Aleister Crowley, a diabolist and self-styled 'wickedest man in the world'), it works because of one of the most moving melodies of any Bowie song. And Bowie, 'playing in a silent film', is setting himself up as the bit-part actor waiting for the starring role.

FILL YOUR HEART

(ROSE/WILLIAMS)

This cover version of a song by American singer-songwriter Biff Rose is another example of Hunky Dory's rather forced jollity. Lyrically almost hippy-like with its talk of 'happiness is here today' and lovers with minds free of 'thoughts unkind', it is downright weird in view of Bowie's own writing, which glorifies individualism and self-absorption. A good pop tune, though, with the strings and piano dominating as usual.

ANDY WARHOL

Never one to hide his influences, Bowie paid homage to three pivotal figures on Hunky Dory. Andy Warhol, by making non-talents into celebrities, showed up the artificiality of image creation, and this idea had an enormous influence on Bowie. The song has some positively vicious Spanish-styled guitar, whip cracks and the kind of effective riff Bowie could rifle off at will during the early Seventies. In 1995, Bowie, clad in Andy's leather jacket and platinum fright-wig, actually got to play the man himself in the film *Basquiat (Build A Fort, Set It On Fire)* and included the song on the Outside tour set-list. Warhol apparently hated the song.

SONG FOR BOB DYLAN

This doesn't really work. Bowie seems unsure whether to go for an outright parody of Dylan or not, but again, like everything on 'Hunky Dory', has a catchy melody and a winning chorus.

QUEEN BITCH

Bowie's scrawly sleeve notes say 'Some V.U. white light returned with thanks', and The Velvet Underground influence is marked on this song, a rollicking, knock-about tale of cross-dressing and gay love set against the *crème de la crème* of campy guitar riffs from Ronno. These were the days when Bowie could relegate songs such as this to mere B-sides. The ever public-fleecing RCA tagged this on to the 'Rebel Rebel' single over two years later.

THE BEWLAY BROTHERS

One of Bowie's most important songs, and undoubtedly the best closure to any Bowie album, this song deals in fictionalised form with the relationship between Bowie and step-brother Terry. The lyrics are full of imagery centered yet again on the malleability and deceptive qualities of the individual: 'Now my brother lays upon the Rocks/He could be dead. He could be not; He could be You', and a homosexual relationship is also implied with the lines: 'In the Crutch-hungry Dark/Was where we flayed our mark'. A remarkable song and, due undoubtedly to the very personal nature of the lyric, to my knowledge never performed live.

BONUS TRACKS ON 1990 RE-ISSUE:

BOMBERS

Poor, mildly embarrassing re-tread of some of the wartime themes of 'Running Gun Blues' with Bowie in cringe-inducing form vocally.

THE SUPERMEN

Alternative version.

QUICKSAND

A demo recording.

THE BEWLAY BROTHERS

An almost identical 'alternative' version to the original and another CD supernumerary.

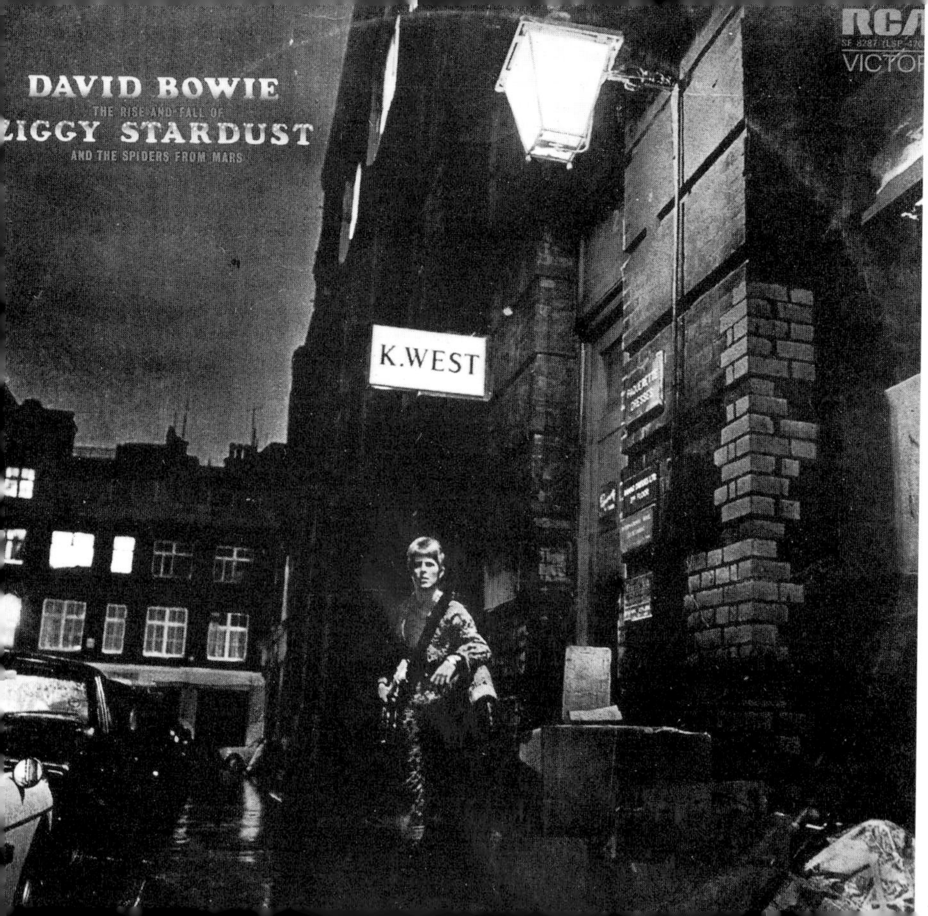
DAVID BOWIE
THE RISE AND FALL OF
ZIGGY STARDUST
AND THE SPIDERS FROM MARS
K.WEST

THE RISE AND FALL OF ZIGGY STARDUST AND THE SPIDERS FROM MARS

(ORIGINAL UK ISSUE: RCA VICTOR R SF 8287, RELEASED 6 JUNE 1972; UK CD: EMI EMC 3577; US SPECIAL EDITION CD: RYKODISC RCD 10134; US SPECIAL EDITION CD: RYKODISC 80134 (ENHANCED 20-BIT MASTER VERSION); UK CHART: 5 [TOTAL WEEKS IN CHART: 172] US CHART: 75)

Despite this album's enormous cultural significance, in many ways 'Ziggy Stardust', again co-produced by Ken Scott, and recorded at Trident Studios, London, now seems like the son of 'Hunky Dory'. Certainly no bad thing, but the album, which hit the shops at about the same time as Roxy Music's début album, sounds almost like a throwback to the Sixties when compared with the extremities and experimentalism of Eno/Ferry and Co. In musical terms, Side 1 in particular moves on very little from a winning formula, and the rock numbers such as 'Suffragette City' are almost tame compared with the glam slam of 'Aladdin Sane'.

Although it is regularly touted as one of pop's great concept albums, telling the tale of the rise and fall of the fictional rocker Ziggy Stardust, there is, in fact, no consistent plot development or narrative structure beyond an opener, which temporally places the events five years from the apocalypse, and an ending which neatly wraps up things with a suicide. An elaborate Ziggy stage show was planned by Bowie in late 1973, with a more developed narrative sketched in, but it never came to fruition.

What Bowie actually did was to collect a portfolio of songs which dealt with stardom and how it is manufactured within the entertainment business. Read like this, the album makes far more sense. 'Star' for example then becomes a shameless exercise in destroying the myth of art for art's sake and reveals the grasping self-promotion that is at the centre of most popular music. 'Starman' loses the comic book sci-fi trappings and becomes a statement about the Messianic quality of our rock idols.

Ziggy Stardust is also heavily laden with images of rock's past, with Hendrix and Bolan making guest appearances. This sense of history, taken together with the album's self-referentiality – a rock star making an album about a rock star – makes Ziggy Stardust, as writer Jon Savage pointed out, pop's first postmodern record. Fact/fiction, past/present are deliberately being played around with in a way new to pop.

And Bowie played the part with tireless aplomb. Soon neither he nor his audience were really sure whether this Kabuki-styled androgyny from Zog was the 'real' Bowie or not. Bowie showed that everyone's personality could indeed be a 'sack of things', and the idea that pop could not only comment on, but enable, these changes became central to how pop would develop from that day on.

FIVE YEARS

A simple drum figure introduces what is arguably the strongest cut on the album, as the narrative locates the action five years from the end of the world. The music moves with Bowie the narrator at a walking pace, and Bowie is once again treading the boards in an imagined real life: 'It was cold and it rained so I felt like an actor'. Swirling violins, impassioned cries, and this pop song, so full of danger and drama, is over.

SOUL LOVE

Only the most tortuous piece of hypothesising could actually fit this particular song into any sort of complete narrative concept. It's still a very fine song indeed, full of remonstrations about the link between secular and non-secular love, and the infectious rhythm, neat pop guitar solo, and sing-a-long-a-Bowie coda make it.

MOONAGE DAYDREAM

This is one of Bowie's best-ever songs, beautifully paced and played. The religiosity of the opening two tracks again resurfaces: 'The church of man-love/ Is such a holy place to be' and Bowie is still playing the sci-fi card for all it's worth ('Put your ray-gun to my head'). It's also noticeable, as journalist Chris Brazier pointed out in a 1976 prize-winning essay, how much Bowie, in an attempt to comment on rock history, utilised slangy, hip Americanisms. 'Moonage Daydream' is a good example of this, filled as it is with lines such as 'Mama-papa', 'freak out', 'lay it [the real thing] on me', and 'rock-and-rolling-bitch'. Ziggy Stardust, despite being regarded as the embodiment of the English obsession with style, is also, at least lyrically, peculiarly Americanised.

STARMAN

Bowie's second UK hit (and the single which really broke him big-time) finally came with this cartoonesque slab of highly contagious pop with its unforgettable chorus. Bowie's fascination with all things galactic tapped into an area of public fascination with sci-fi hitherto unexplored within popular music, although undoubtedly part of the national psyche, as the success of TV programmes such as Dr Who proved. Here the arrival of the Ziggy figure, who, in another bout of Americanism, thinks he'll 'blow your minds', is equated with the second coming of Christ, and Bowie neatly draws attention to the Messianic qualities of superstardom. Anyone around in the Seventies will never forget Bowie's appearance on *Top Of The Pops*, crimson of hair, pallid of complexion and pally of demeanour, a lovingly limp wrist dangling over Mick Ronson's shoulder.

IT AIN'T EASY

(DAVIES)

This cover of a little-known Ron Davies song just doesn't fit in and its inclusion on the album is doubly puzzling given the stock-pile of excellence Bowie had at the time.

LADY STARDUST

Another effective piano part dominates this undemanding piece of pop. 'Lady Stardust' takes Marc Bolan and his myth as subject matter and thus continues the idea of the album as a sort of self-referential universe dominated by fictionalised accounts of rock's real-life history.

STAR

Backing vocals like air-raid sirens, a hammering piano and the best lyric on the album make this a pivotal song in the Bowie canon. Here Bowie's lyric embodies his obsession with notoriety ('So inviting – so enticing to play the part'), and the hard-headed commercialism ('I could do with the money') behind pop's façade of integrity and authenticity.

HANG ON TO YOURSELF

Again the acoustic, rather than lead, guitar hogs the limelight in this out-and-out rocker. It's as if Bowie can't sonically distance himself from the singer-songwriting pretensions of the previous 'Hunky Dory' version of Bowie. That said, it is a fabulous song with another fine guitar break from Ronson. The 'Come on' exhortation at the end is almost coital in its repeated delivery.

ZIGGY STARDUST

During the early Seventies Bowie was so adroit at writing instantly recognisable and skilful pop/rock riffs, and nowhere is there a better example than on this, the title track of the album. Like Jimi Hendrix, Ziggy 'played it left hand/But made it too far' and, in what many take to be a reference to the fans who helped provide Hendrix with the drugs that would eventually kill him, Bowie sings 'When the kids had killed the man/I had to break up the band'. There is also a powerful sense of drama at the song's dénouement, when the band cuts off before the final 'Ziggy played guitar' salvo. That said, this studio version, like so much on the album, sounds unsuitably restrained and polite.

SUFFRAGETTE CITY

This is another 'lost' Bowie single, which was coupled with 'Stay' and released in Britain to promote the hits compilation 'ChangesBowie' in 1976. It was a complete flop, not even denting the lower reaches of the Top 75. That said, this tale of a hot and bothered Bowie fending off his male lover while his female one 'said she had to squeeze it but she... and then she' remained a live favourite over three decades and the 'Wham bam thank you mam' is still naughty, but nice.

ROCK'N'ROLL SUICIDE

Not content to wait for the 'Diamond Dogs' material to be completed, RCA turned this, perhaps Bowie's most dramatic moment ever, into a minor hit single (UK Number 22) and thus once again short-changed Bowie fans, many of whom would literally buy an EP of his selected sneezing at this stage. (Remember, 'The Laughing Gnome' had just sold well over a quarter of a million copies in the UK alone).

'Rock'n'Roll Suicide' is an effective parody of the sort of Las Vegas show business schmaltz Bowie found so execrable. Pounding away at the 'Gimme your hands 'cos you're wonderful' line, he lashes out at the light entertainment 'you were a lovely audience' rhetoric to great effect.

BONUS TRACKS ON 1990 RE-ISSUE:

JOHN I'M ONLY DANCING

In this, one of his most overtly gay songs, Bowie assures his male lover that he is only flirting with the opposite sex. Bowie had famously admitted to being gay in an interview with *Melody Maker*'s Michael Watts in January 1972. This admission not only secured him the tabloid publicity to make him a star, but also, very importantly, as the first instance of a male pop star being open about the gay side of his sexuality, helped others who felt themselves to be on the margins to take centre stage and admit their true orientation. Although Bowie was later branded a closet homophobe by certain gay critics, this initial stance was tremendously important, and the fact that a song such as this reached Number 12 in the UK Charts is of great cultural significance. It's also a damn fine pop song, and one of his best-ever singles. Originally released four months after the 'Ziggy Stardust' album hit the racks, this 1979 re-mix makes for a welcome addition on this CD, although yet another version, with saxophone well to the fore, recorded during the 'Aladdin Sane' sessions and included on initial pressings of the 'Changes One Bowie' compilation, is even better. The Aladdin Sane-era version can now be found on Rykodisc's 'Sound + Vision' boxed set.

VELVET GOLDMINE

This was originally to be found (without Bowie's permission) along with 'Changes' on the flip side of the UK re-issue of 'Space Oddity' in 1975.

SWEET HEAD

An interesting piece for Bowie completists, it's got more of an r'n'b influence than the rest of the Ziggy-era material, and the lyrics would undoubtedly have caused ructions at the Beeb if the song had ever been aired.

ZIGGY STARDUST

A weak demo recording, but if EMI/Rykodisc say we've got to have it, then have it we must. It's not even as if these demos show the song in an interesting state of unreadiness. They sound as if Bowie is still in a condition of extreme panic, and the vocals bring to mind the words 'sheep' and 'bleating'.

LADY STARDUST

Again a demo version. You have been warned.

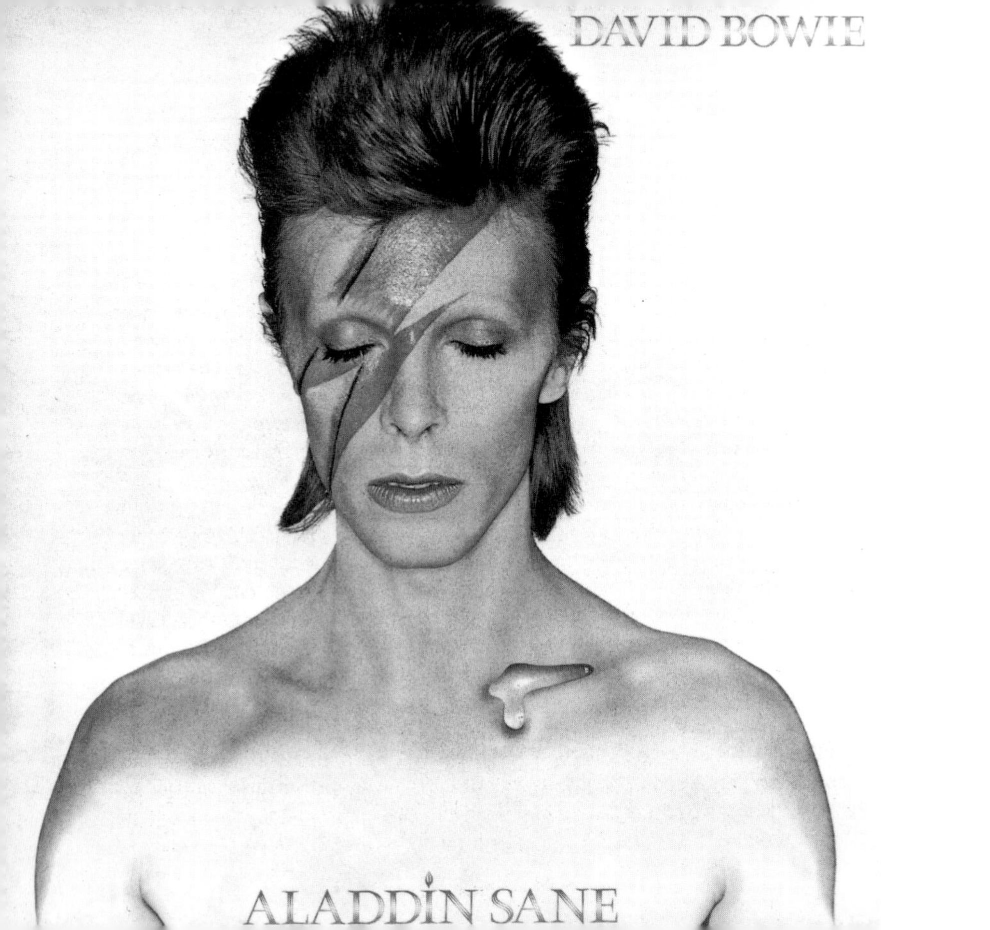
DAVID BOWIE
ALADDIN SANE

ALADDIN SANE

(ORIGINAL UK ISSUE: RCA VICTOR RS 1001, RELEASED 13 APRIL 1973; UK CD: EMI EMC 3579; US CD: RYKODISC RCD 10153; UK CHART: 1 [TOTAL WEEKS IN CHART: 72]; US CHART: 17 [8])

Regarded at the time as something of a let-down after 'Ziggy', 'Aladdin Sane', although conceptually weaker and perhaps not as consistent in terms of overall quality, should now be regarded as the definitive glam-rock Bowie album. The band are altogether more daring: Ronson's guitar is prominent and high in the mix and Mike Garson's manically jazzy piano further broadens the musical canvas. Bowie's songs show a strong determination to break free from the neat 'Hunky-Doryisms' of old, particularly on the epically-fractured title track and gorgeously melodramatic 'Time'. Again it's co-produced by Bowie and Ken Scott (who was becoming, as Bowie later commented, his George Martin figure).

The album is also more informed, as Bowie was later to comment, by the spirit of rock-and-roll, thus making the more experimental sections even more audacious in comparison. Mostly written during the latter half of 1972 on tour in America, much of the material has a more strident r'n'b sensibility, not least the album's biggest hit 'The Jean Genie'. Aladdin Sane was, after all, as Bowie claimed, 'Ziggy goes to America'. Although in many ways the playful theatricality of his work makes him the product of a typically English sensibility, Bowie had long been influenced by American rockers, and on this album he took the traditions of Americana and gave them a peculiarly parochial spin.

'Aladdin Sane' was released during a period when Bowie's commercial and artistic stock, at least on the home front, had never been higher. He had already earned a reputation as pop-resuscitator by helping to produce albums for the ailing Mott The Hoople ('All The Young Dudes'), Lou Reed (the really excellent 'Transformer') and Iggy and the Stooges ('Raw Power') and, after almost ten years of trying, had finally won mainstream acceptance, at least in Britain. Looking back at the version of Bowie at the time – a war-painted sex-change harlequin with a fast growing repertoire of songs concerning galactic apocalypse, head-fuck, suicide and 'tri-sexuality' – one might reasonably wonder how on earth he became the biggest mainstream commercial success of 1973. In fact it's not so difficult to see why. Musically, Bowie had a locker-full of soaring, catchy melodies still conventional enough for your Dad to whistle along to. And, perhaps more importantly, his work was at the very core of English pop sensibility, re-articulating, in an admittedly extreme manner, the British love for theatricality and make-up. 'Aladdin Sane' is the album in which these stylisations work the best.

This time there are no bonus tracks, even though bootleggers have been peddling an instrumental 'Love Aladdin Vein' (which would later form the basis of 'Sweet Thing') and another song, 'Tired Of My Life' (a precursor to Scary Monster's 'It's No Game'), for years.

WATCH THAT MAN

Musically this is a good example of the way in which Bowie's rock tracks were now more up-front and r'n'b influenced, with Ronson's lead guitar so high in the mix that Bowie's vocals are drowned out. Another killer chorus made this one of his finest rock songs, and pianist Mike Garson again adds that special touch.

ALADDIN SANE (1913-1938-197?)

This is arguably the album's most outstanding track, with Bowie's vocals beautifully poised and Garson's truly manic piano showing how effective a soloist he can be. The title is, of course, a pun, and was originally 'Love Aladdin Vain', or 'Vein' thus referencing drug use rather than madness.

DRIVE IN SATURDAY

Bowie has always been interested in fracturing time, in looking at the future in terms of the past. On 'Drive In Saturday' the future is one in which sex has to be re-learned through watching old films: 'When people stared in Jagger's eyes and scored/Like the video films we saw'. It's one of Bowie's all-time catchiest melodies, suitably melding Fifties doo-wap with Seventies pop, and the single justifiably soared to Number 3 in the UK during the spring of 1973.

PANIC IN DETROIT

Bowie's Seventies music was all about alien states, and, in America, Bowie had found one just across the pond. In 1993 Bowie commented: 'Here was this alternative world that I'd been talking about and it had all the violence and all the strangeness and bizarreness and it was really happening. Suddenly my songs didn't look out of place'. Ronson's guitar is even more blues-influenced and the soon-to-be-famous backing singer Linda Lewis providing a hint of what was to come on Young Americans.

CRACKED ACTOR

A devilish track. Bowie's obsession with stardom is brilliantly captured on this grungy blues cut replete with 'authentic' harmonica and a cod daddy-o blues progression from Ronson. Bowie's muse projects him twenty-five years into the future as a redundant, fucked-up, ex-movie star, bloated and gloating, enmeshed in the trappings of his own washed-out stardom. The line 'forget that I'm fifty 'cos you just got paid' now has a most bizarre ring to it.

TIME

Not only is this one of the few pop songs to include the word 'wanking' and get away with it, it is another highly inventive track. Musically this is simply soaring, with Garson's piano and Ronson's guitar again dominating, and Bowie's overwrought vocal again perfect for the melodrama. Ronson's little appropriation of Beethoven's Ninth, Bowie's signature tune for the 'Aladdin Sane' tour in the Walter/Wendy Carlos guise, is the album's best musical moment. The 'Billy Doll' mentioned in the lyric is the late Billy Murcia, original drummer with The New York Dolls who O.D.'ed in London in November 1972.

THE PRETTIEST STAR

Bowie had originally released this, reputedly about his soon-to-be wife Angie, as a single in 1970 with Marc Bolan on guitar. That rather limp version was beefed up for this album cut, and again Bowie injects a dose of Fifties doo-wop into the mix. Pretty, but probably the album's least interesting moment, although as a companion piece to 'Cracked Actor', this time casting his beloved in the wholesome role of a glittering Lilian Gish-like starlet, it's effective enough.

LET'S SPEND THE NIGHT TOGETHER

Bowie acknowledges the album's main area of indebtedness with this zapped-up and arguably superior version of the 1966 Stones single.

THE JEAN GENIE

A perfect rock/pop artefact, this Jagger/Richards-inspired song narrowly missed the top spot in the UK in early 1973. Culturally significant in that its title is not only a shamanistic pun on the Genie of the lamp, and thus keeps up the Aladdin pantomime references (with all the cross-dressing inherent therein), it also references the underground gay politico author Jean Genet.

LADY GRINNING SOUL

Sensuous and beautiful, this depiction of the preamble to love-making is intense in its honesty and quite incongruous within the Bowie canon. Again, Mike Garson's piano is in the starring role, imbuing the music with a refined Continental touch, and the whole makes for a glittering ending to a fine album.

PIN-UPS

(ORIGINAL UK ISSUE: RCA VICTOR RS 1003, RELEASED 19 OCTOBER 1973; UK CD: EMI EMC 3580; US CD: RYKODISC RCD 10136; UK CHART: 1 [TOTAL WEEKS IN CHART: 37]; US CHART: 23 [9])

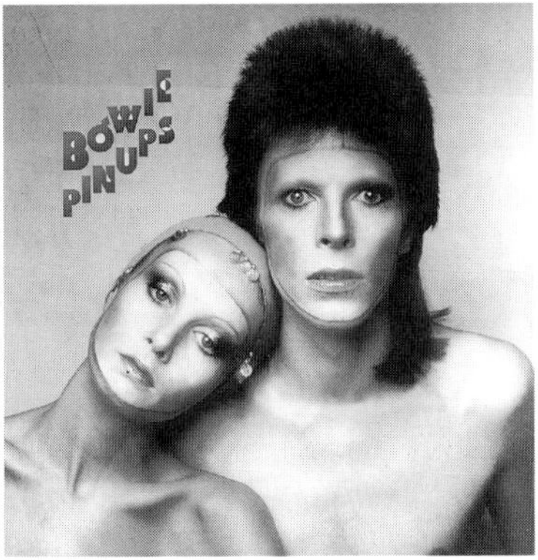

Actually Ziggy hadn't broken up the band – at least not yet. Unsure of his next move after the 'retirement' gig in early July, and under pressure from RCA for new product, Bowie took the Spiders minus drummer Woody Woodmansey to the Château d'Herouville studios in France to record 'Pin-Ups' as an interim measure.

By 1973, rock's history was almost twenty years long and already there were signs of revivalist notions. British glam rock itself was full of Fifties re-runs. On the one hand there was Roxy Music who often brilliantly re-invoked Fifties kitsch for their Seventies vignettes. Then there was glam rock's pop side with groups such as Showaddywaddy,

The Rubettes and Mud all repackaging nostalgia for the pre-teenies. 'Pin-Ups', a collection of covers of Bowie's favourites from the London scene between 1964 and 1967, like Bryan Ferry's 'These Foolish Things' released earlier in 1973, rode the Zeitgeist of British pop history's first real wave of retroactivity and made an effortless début at Number 1 in the UK.

The album does sound good now in its remastered form and it swings along at a fine pace, with each song segueing neatly into the next. Produced by Bowie and Ken Scott, the band was essentially the old Spiders unit, with Wood-mansey replaced by Aynsley Dunbar on drums.

However, the album is, in truth, a pretty dispensable affair. Bowie's still reedy vocal is unsuited to the rock attack of The Who's 'Anyway, Anyhow, Anywhere', and he's even less at ease with the hip r'n'b revivalism of The Mojos and The Pretty Things. For many fans, these clod-hopping tracks sounded like ancient history compared with the increasing sophistication of Bowie's own original compositions. When he moves on to more whimsical pop, as in the cover of The Kinks' 'Where Have All the Good Times Gone', or the hammy, neo-classical version of Pink Floyd's psychedelic anthem 'See Emily Play', he's on safer ground. The album's highlight is, of course, his cover of The Merseys' 'Sorrow', the only moment when he vastly improves on the original. This, the album's only single release, became one of his biggest hits, reaching Number 3 in Britain and staying in the charts for 15 weeks. Since that track graces a number of Bowie 'Best Of' compilations, 'Pin-Ups' itself, despite the 1990 reissue containing the rousing 'Port Of Amsterdam' as a bonus track, remains one for Bowie nuts only.

ROSALYN

(JIMMY DUNCAN/ BILL FARLEY)

Bowie is nothing if not a pop *aficionado,* as evidenced by this unearthing of a Number 41 hit by The Pretty Things. It's a riffy if unremarkable song.

HERE COMES THE NIGHT

(BERT BERNS)

Originally a Number 2 hit in 1965 by Them, this gets the full honking Bowie sax treatment and contains one of the album's standout moments with Bowie's opening yodelling scream.

I WISH YOU WOULD

(BILLY ARNOLD)

Originally by The Yardbirds, this is where Bowie really shows himself up as a wooden and limited r'n'b singer.

SEE EMILY PLAY

(SYD BARRETT)

The original by Syd Barrett's Pink Floyd (and the distinction is important) reached Number 6 in 1967. It's one of British psychedelia's signature songs and Bowie does it proud with some 'Bewlay Brothers'-styled cockney for the choruses and an overblown classical flourish at the end.

EVERYTHING'S ALRIGHT

(CROUCH/KONRAD/STAVELY/JAMES/KARLSON)

Boring re-run of a Mojos 1964 hit.

I CAN'T EXPLAIN

(PETE TOWNSHEND)

Slowed-down sax-driven version of The Who's first hit included on the set list of some of the early Serious Moonlight concerts a decade later.

FRIDAY ON MY MIND

(YOUNG/VANDA)

Bowie's in Anthony Newley mode yet again for this cover of The Easybeats' 1966 hit.

SORROW

(FELDMAN/GOLDSTEIN/GOTTEHRER)

A great Bowie single and far and away the album's highlight – lush strings, beautifully paced sax solo and a fine vocal performance. It was originally a Number 4 hit for The Merseys in 1966.

DON'T BRING ME DOWN

(JONNIE DEE)

Superfluous cover of a 1964 Top 10 hit for The Pretty Things.

SHAPES OF THINGS

(SAMWELL-SMITH/MCCARTY/RELF)

The futurism of this 1966 Top 3 hit for The Yardbirds obviously appealed to Bowie, but it's hard not to conclude that in the intervening years his own songs had revisited similar themes with far more telling effect.

ANYWAY, ANYHOW, ANYWHERE

(PETE TOWNSHEND/ROGER DALTREY)

Bowie's vocals had yet to undergo the transformation which would make him in the mid-Seventies a genuinely technically great vocalist. Here he's straining and can't match Roger Daltrey for dynamic attack on this cover of The Who's second UK hit from May 1965.

WHERE HAVE ALL THE GOOD TIMES GONE

(RAY DAVIES)

Absolutely fine cover of a Kinks song, and the suitably fatalistic lyrics fit 'Pin-Ups'' nostalgia trip perfectly.

BONUS TRACKS ON 1990 RE-ISSUE:

GROWIN' UP

(BRUCE SPRINGSTEEN)

Given all that Bruce Springsteen would go on to stand for as the decade unravelled, the arch-poseur's interest in the 'Honest Joe-isms' of the Boss appear ludicrous. This is a pretty perfunctory cover too. Along with this track, Bowie also recorded a version of the Velvet Underground's 'White Light/White Heat' and The Beach Boys' 'God Only Knows' for an aborted PinUps II featuring American cover versions.

PORT OF AMSTERDAM

(JACQUES BREL/M. SHUMAN)

Bowie gives a stirring performance on this cover of a Jacques Brel song, originally the B-side to the 'Sorrow' single.

Bowie
DIAMOND DOGS

DIAMOND DOGS

(ORIGINAL UK ISSUE: RCA VICTOR APLI 0576, RELEASED 24 APRIL 1974; UK CD: EMI EMC 3584; US CD: RYKODISC RCD 10137; UK CHART: 1 [TOTAL WEEKS IN CHART: 32]; US CHART: 5 [10])

Now bereft of The Spiders, Bowie was truly a solo artist once again, and 'Diamond Dogs', recorded late in 1973 and early 1974, shows Bowie both at his most indulgent and at his most creative. Far from being the *folie de grandeur* which many critics have suggested, the album encapsulates what truly makes him tick. It is a masterpiece of invention, cinematic in its scope, breathtakingly audacious in its execution and, finally, scary as hell. It also single-handedly brought the glam rock era to a close. After 'Diamond Dogs' there was nothing more to do, no way forward which would not result in self-parody or crass repetition.

Produced by Bowie, engineered and, in part, mixed by Mike Harwood, it shows Bowie taking on the role of lead guitarist whilst pianist Mike Garson is once again on hand to add a touch of eccentricity. Tony Visconti, then building his own recording studio, and having freed himself from the task of producing Marc Bolan's increasingly formulaic pop, was reconciled with Bowie and was brought in to arrange the strings for '1984' and to mix the album.

Bowie had originally intended to produce a musical of the classic George Orwell novel 1984, but when Orwell's widow refused him the rights, he found himself with a collection of songs dealing with the apocalyptic totalitarian themes of the book and nowhere to put them. He therefore created his own future urban nightmare environment, Hunger City, a sort of post-nuclear, technologically primitive hell populated by tribes of proto-punks looting their way through the streets. Again, as with Ziggy, the actual narrative remains under-developed. Like all of Bowie's best work there are plenty of unanswered questions, gaps and contradictions to allow listeners to construct their own meaning of events.

The music on the album is densely packed with piano, strings, sax, synths and guitars melding together beautifully, particularly on the criminally underrated 'Sweet Thing'. *Melody*

Maker's Chris Charlesworth noted that 'For most of the tracks, he's adopted a 'wall of sound' technique borrowed not a little from Phil Spector'. Bowie's songwriting had also become influenced by the cut-up technique, pioneered in literature by the American writers William Burroughs and Brion Gysin. The lyrics are now consciously more fractured and less figurative as images collide with each other in a spiralling non-sequential private universe. The spoken narrative of 'Future Legend' is particularly Burroughsian, reading like an off-cut from *Naked Lunch*. A remarkable work and probably Bowie's finest album from the Seventies.

The cover art work by Guy Peellaert, which showed Bowie as half Ziggy/half dog, caused a minor rumpus when it was noticed that the dog's donger was in full view. The albums were recalled by RCA for the offending member to be airbrushed out, although a few originals slipped through the net to become collectors' items. The EMI/Rykodisc re-issued CD now comes with the original art work fully restored, balls and all.

FUTURE LEGEND

The tone is immediately set by this minute-long narrative introduction in which Bowie details the horrors of Hunger City: 'Fleas the size of rats sucked on rats the size of cats'. The opening hyena-like howl is both as chill a moment as any committed to tape by Bowie and a demonstration of the camp, kitsch-like quality of Bowie's cartoonesque imagery.

DIAMOND DOGS

Musically this title track plods along rather unimaginatively and is undoubtedly the album's weakest moment. It does allow Bowie the chance for yet more canine vocalisations and continues the narrative with the introduction of the Halloween Jack character. For Hunger City, Bowie had drawn on a story his father, who worked for Barnado's children's homes, had told him about the visit of Lord Shaftesbury to poverty-stricken areas of London where he found children in rags living on the rooftops. Hence Halloween Jack 'lives on top of Manhattan Chase'.

SWEET THING/ CANDIDATE/SWEET THING (REPRISE)

The album's high-spot. As a piece of music this is seamless and dramatic, showcasing a new maturity in Bowie's work. 'Sweet Thing' opens with Bowie's vocal deep and growling, and builds, courtesy of Garson's finest performance yet, into a seedy ballad of prostitution and druggy Americanised low-life. 'Candidate', originally a song in its own right and included as a bonus track on the CD re-issue, is here much-changed and contains some of Bowie's most powerful writing: 'We'll buy some drugs and watch a band/And jump in a river holding hands' before segueing neatly into a reprised 'Sweet Thing'.

REBEL REBEL

Who says Bowie can't play guitar? The last of his bona fide glam singles, it is in essence a superior re-write of 'Jean Genie' and thus one of the few examples of truly formulaic pop in the Bowie canon. Bowie is definitely writing another mini-manifesto for all the Bowie Boys and Bowie Girls, who were one of the most conspicuous aspects of pre-punk youth culture, and the lines 'You got your mother in a whirl/She's not sure if you're a boy or a girl' sum up early - '70s gender-bending perfectly.

ROCK'N'ROLL WITH ME

There are definite hints of Bowie's 'plastic soul' phase, particularly in the infectious piano part, in this cute pop song which builds to the kind of rousing chorus he would have given his eye-teeth to come up with ten years later.

WE ARE THE DEAD

After two plain pop songs we're back, courtesy of a keyboard line straight out of a horror movie score, into the doomy dystopia of *1984*. Bowie here is identifying with the plight of Winston Smith, the central character in the Orwell novel, and, after an illicit sexual affair, his inevitable re-assimilation into the totalitarian state. RCA were later to release the track as the B-side of 'TVC 15' in yet another exercise in short-changing the fan.

1984

In 1971 Isaac Hayes helped kick-start what later became known as disco music with his theme tune to the film *Shaft*. Bowie borrows heavily from that track's guitar work and, together with some on-the-button Philly strings, provides the clearest clue yet of his upcoming disco phase. The song was covered by the resurrected Tina Turner on her 'Private Dancer' album of 1984, a bizarre choice of song for that most middle-of-the-road of soul-stresses, filled as it is with gloomy predictions for the future of mankind.

BIG BROTHER/CHANT OF THE EVER CIRCLING SKELETAL FAMILY

In which Bowie returns once again to the idea of the 'strong man', the 'homo superior', as a means of salvation, this time through taking on the Big Brother of the Orwell novel, whose totalitarian grip was ultimately absolute. It was this fascination with supermen of one persuasion or another, whether it be his own fictionalised rock personae, or the figures of myth, legend, philosophy (through an interest in Nietzsche) or novels, which would culminate in Bowie's own delusions of grandeur during his flirtation with Nazi-chic two years later. With hindsight, we can all see it coming. Whatever, 'Big Brother' is a daring, insistent, somehow frightening paean to the Super God, and the way in which it segues into the 'Chant Of The Ever Circling Skeletal Family' (a truly mesmeric and frightening chant in 5/4 time) is one of the greatest moments Bowie has committed to tape.

BONUS TRACKS ON 1990 RE-ISSUE:

DODO

Between 18 and 20 October 1973 at the London Marquee, Bowie recorded The Midnight Special for US TV, showcasing material from his just-released 'Pin-Ups' album, featuring a duet with Marianne Faithfull, tastefully attired in a nun's habit slashed at the back to reveal her derriere. The show was aired on NBC but has never been shown on British terrestrial television. 'Dodo' (then entitled 'You Didn't Hear It From Me') was performed as part of a medley with '1984'. Quite weak and one for completists only.

CANDIDATE (DEMO VERSION)

This, however, is probably the best bonus track unearthed by Rykodisc for the re-issues. A long, piano-led song with a fine melody and one of Bowie's naughtiest couplets ('Inside every teenage girl there's a fountain/Inside every young pair of pants there's a mountain'). In the re-written version which appeared on 'Diamond Dogs', Bowie was to up the ante on this rather playful sexual innuendo considerably.

DAVID LIVE

(ORIGINAL UK ISSUE: RCA VICTOR APL 2 0771, RELEASED 29 OCTOBER 1974; UK CD: EMI DBLD 1; US CD: RYKODISC RCD 1038/39; UK CHART: 2 [TOTAL WEEKS IN CHART: 12]; US CHART: 8 [8])

In April 1974 Bowie left England for the States to launch what is now regarded as one of the most theatrical and elaborate tours ever attempted. As the cover shot for the 'David Live' album shows, the Diamond Dogs Revue revealed Bowie ashen and painfully thin, the Ziggy crop discarded in favour of a peroxide-orange parting and the Kabuki trappings of yore replaced by suits and braces. With Mick Ronson gone and The Spiders a fast-fading memory, Bowie assumed the mantel of Diamond Dogs' central character Halloween Jack in what was, in essence, a one-man show. On stage he performed in a re-creation of the album's 'Hunger City', a kind of Fritz Lang's *Metropolis* meets George Orwell's *1984*, all decaying skyscrapers and crumbling bridgeheads.

For 'Space Oddity' he was lofted several rows out above the audience by a cherry-picker crane, and sang the song into a microphone masquerading as a telephone. Annoyingly, due to a crackly line, that particular song is not to be found on the album.

David Live' can only give an aural, and therefore partial, idea of what must have been a fascinating rock theatre experience. Only Alan Yentob's brilliant Omnibus documentary *Cracked Actor* gives any taste of what this stunning revue must have looked like. David, if you've got any tapes of your Seventies shows in the vaults, please release them! According to Kevin Cann's excellent *David Bowie: A Chronology* UK promoters turned down the chance to stage the tour at the Empire Pool, Wembley, because Bowie's management Mainman were demanding around £7.00 a ticket, then an unacceptably high price.

'David Live', released at the beginning of Bowie's coked-out cabaret phase, is a tense, unnerving album. His vocals seem cracked and tired, and the band, fronted by guitarist Earl Slick, give an often less than commanding performance. This was not surprising since, on the night it was recorded, they were in dispute over money and unhappy about being asked to play every night behind screens in order that the chilling calm of Hunger City was not ruined by the presence of a bass amp stage left. Bowie, himself, has been dismissive of the album, even going as far as to refer to it as 'David Dead'! It does, nevertheless, contain some fine performances, notably an intriguing cabaret version of 'All The Young Dudes', a brilliantly re-worked 'Width Of A Circle' and a marvellously overwrought and slowed-down version of the epic 'Rock'n'Roll Suicide'. 'Knock On Wood' (a UK Top 10 single, backed with a live version of 'Panic In Detroit' not included as a bonus track on this CD re-issue), a cover of the old Steve Cropper and Eddie Floyd rhythm-and-blues classic, points to the future direction Bowie's own music would soon take, along with the valuable addition of the bonus track 'Here Today, Gone Tomorrow'.

Tracks, Disc 1: '1984', 'Rebel Rebel', 'Moonage Daydream', 'Sweet Thing', 'Changes', 'Suffragette City', 'Aladdin Sane', 'All The Young Dudes', 'Cracked Actor', 'Rock'n'Roll With Me', 'Watch That Man';
Disc 2: 'Knock On Wood', 'Diamond Dogs', 'Big Brother', 'Width Of A Circle', 'Jean Genie', 'Rock'n'Roll Suicide', 'Band Intro', 'Here Today, Gone Tomorrow', 'Time'.

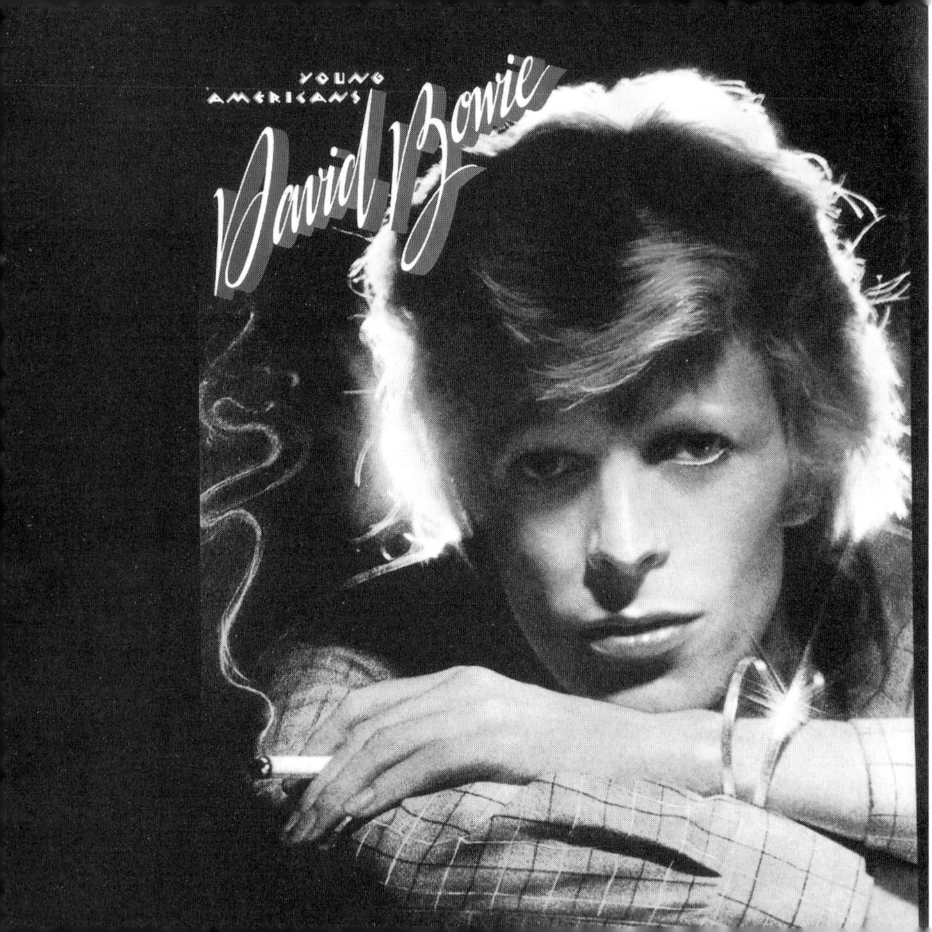
YOUNG AMERICANS
David Bowie

YOUNG AMERICANS

ORIGINAL UK ISSUE: RCA VICTOR RS 1006, RELEASED 7 MARCH 1975; UK CD: EMI EMD 1021; US CD: RYKODISC RCD 10140; UK CHART: 2 [TOTAL WEEKS IN CHART: 13]; US CHART: 9 [17])

During late-summer break in the Diamond Dogs Review, Bowie decamped to Philadelphia and the Sigma Sound Studios to record one of the most influential albums of the Seventies. 1974 was the year that disco music, hitherto the preserve of gay and Latino communities, broke big with US Number 1's in the shape of the Hues Corporation's 'Rock The Boat' and George McCrae's 'Rock Your Baby'. Bowie's conversion to disco/soul, although perplexing at the time and certainly an audacious step, was not quite as unforeseen as certain critics were wont to portray it. Both 'Aladdin Sane' and 'Diamond Dogs' had displayed a rougher r'n'b slant, and '1984' off the latter was a clear sign of his future direction. Disco also had many things in common with glam rock. Both had attracted the marginalised in society; with glam it was the sexual experimenters, with disco it was women, gays and blacks. Both sets of fans were narcissistic and embraced consumerism in a way progressive rock or folk fans would have baulked at. This fitted in well with Bowie's stance.

Bowie assembled a bona fide r'n'b band including bassist Willy Weeks and saxophonist David Sanborn. His knack for unearthing new talent still hadn't deserted him and a young soul singer called Luther Vandross, called in as backing singer, co-wrote one of the album's best tracks, 'Fascination'. 'Young Americans' was a calculated attempt, after years of relative commercial failure, to produce a hit album in the States, and, although Bowie was to lose a sizeable part of his British following in the process, that is exactly what he got.

With hindsight 'Young Americans' is a curious album; in places it now sounds like an authentic musical reconstruction of then-current black sounds; in others it sounds a most parochial oddity as Bowie's self-conscious jiving betrays a stylised English manner. Dubbing the album 'plastic soul', Bowie argued that this was a peculiarly contrived version of the real thing: "It's the phoniest R&B I've ever heard... If I ever would have got my hands on that record when I was growing up I would have cracked it over my knee."

However, by crossing over into disco/soul music he helped pave the way for the greater commercial success later in the decade of The Bee Gees, although Scotland's Average White Band, now decamped to New York, had beaten Bowie to the punch by enjoying a Number 1 hit with the dance instrumental 'Pick Up The Pieces' the previous year. The Bowie model of white blue-eyed soul was re-hashed, with ever-lessening artistic dividends, by the likes of ABC, Spandau Ballet and Simply Red as the Eighties unwound, and British soul boys and girls everywhere have this pioneering album to thank.

Months after finishing the album, Bowie, without producer Tony Visconti's knowledge, played around with the finished tapes and added the fruits of a spontaneous recording session with John Lennon – the US Number 1 hit 'Fame' and the Lennon/Beatles cover 'Across The Universe'. Lennon also gave Bowie some good advice on how to sort out his managerial problems which appears to have stood him in good stead ever since.

The re-issued version of the album now has three bonus tracks included (originally to be found on the master tapes of an earlier version of the album called 'The Gouster').

YOUNG AMERICANS

Bowie kicks off proceedings with a frantic reconstruction of the mundane nature of American everyday life. Bowie's lyrics sound second-hand, as if they are an imagined version of American exotica, and the band, with a groovy sax-line well to the front, swings along with an almost Latin rhythm. Released as the album's first single it reached Number 18 in the UK and Number 28 in the US.

WIN

'Win' is the sole really outstanding track on the album, with Bowie beginning the process of unearthing his 'true' self after years of role-playing. When he sings 'Well you've never seen me naked and white' you can hear the struggle between the distanced, contrived posturer and a newer, 'real version'. A haunting melody, rippling synth refrain, and some melting backing vocals give this exercise in positivity – 'All you've got to do is win' – a haunting quality, and the resigned vocals betray an uncertainty at odds with the song's message.

FASCINATION

(BOWIE/VANDROSS)

This track has benefited most from the CD remastering and, in fact, appears completely remixed: the sound is now expansive and echoey, giving this dance-floor work-out a new sheen. There's a great riff too and Bowie's cod soul boy routine is coming along a treat: 'Fascination/ Sho'nuff/ Takes a part of me'.

RIGHT

'Right' is undoubtedly the most authentically blue-eyed cut on the album, with Bowie and backing singers bouncing off each other in true call-and-response style. The message merely reiterates the central arse-kicking theme of the previous two tracks as Bowie, now descending into the mire personally, is recognising the signs of collapse.

SOMEBODY UP THERE LIKES ME

Lyrically this is one of Bowie's finest songs, containing a typically disingenuous critique of the corrupting powers of the media, disingenuous in that here Bowie is criticising the very image of what he has purposely become: 'There was a time when we judged a man by what he'd done/ Now we pick them off the screen/What they look like/Where they've been'. Some great sax too.

ACROSS THE UNIVERSE

(LENNON/MCCARTNEY)

This beefed-up funk version of a 1970 Beatles song has typically overblown Bowie vocals, but the song itself isn't particularly suited to Bowie's voice (or personality) and the overall result is unsatisfactory.

CAN YOU HEAR ME

A swooning, yearning song which teeters at times on the verge of cliché, and came as a huge shock to those space cadets still fired-up from the full-tilt pop/rock of the previous year's 'Rebel Rebel'. One of Bowie's most conventional songs, it provides further evidence of his continued fascination with the real and the imaginary, with the admission that he still might simply be 'fakin' it all'.

FAME

(BOWIE, LENNON, ALOMAR)

Bowie's big US breakthrough came courtesy of this commentary on the pressures and pains of stardom. Alomar's infectious riff, created by Alomar for Bowie's own version of The Flare's 'Footstompin'' (1961), is the perfect foil for Bowie's catalogue of evils and woes: 'Fame, what you want is in your limo/Fame, what you get is no tomorrow'.

BONUS TRACKS ON 1991 RE-ISSUE:

WHO CAN I BE NOW?

The music Bowie mistakenly left off the first time round is even more soul-influenced. A sax solo opens this cut, which again deals with a much-used Bowie theme of identity construction.

IT'S GONNA BE ME

This sprawling, heart-wrenching soul ballad was performed late in 1974 when the Diamond Dogs Revue morphed into the Philly Dogs tour, the elaborate set dismantled and Bowie presented as a born-again hipster. Again, pretty essential stuff.

JOHN, I'M ONLY DANCING AGAIN

Released as a single at the end of the '70s, this is a totally re-worked version of the 1972 single, with David Sanborn's sax high in the mix. It reached Number 12 in the UK charts.

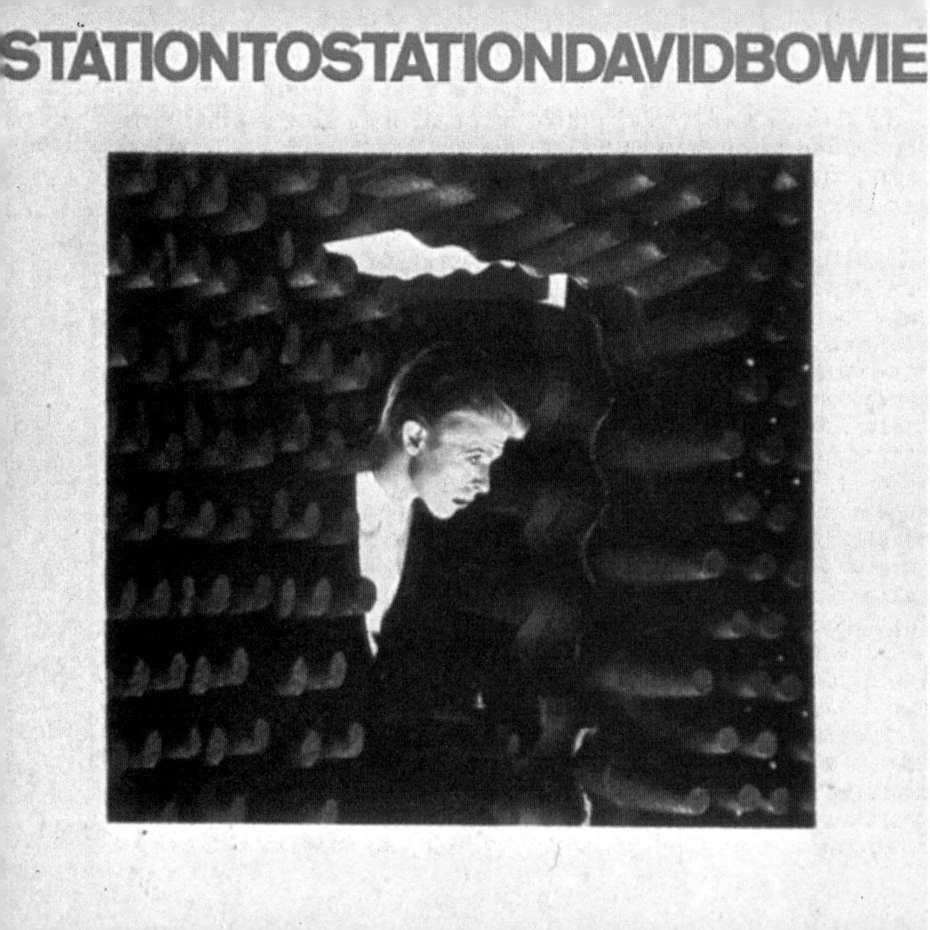
STATIONTOSTATIONDAVIDBOWIE

STATION TO STATION

(ORIGINAL UK ISSUE: RCA VICTOR APLI 1327, RELEASED 23 JANUARY 1976; UK CD: EMI EMD 1020; US CD: RYKODISC RCD 10141; UK CHART: 5 [TOTAL WEEKS IN CHART: 17]; US CHART: 3 [13])

In 1975 Bowie famously pronounced rock dead. 'It's a toothless old woman', he cried, 'I've rocked my last roll'. During the summer he completed work on his first, and probably still best, major film to date, *The Man Who Fell To Earth*. In this cult sci-fi classic Bowie plays the role of an alien who is forced to come to Earth in the search for resources for his dying planet, falls prey to mankind's corruption and is unable to return. Bowie imbued the role with a frozen demeanour and he brought the same sense of detachment and rootlessness to his next musical project.

Originally entitled 'The Return Of The Thin White Duke', this was, for almost twenty years, the last album to feature Bowie in character and it was his least sympathetic character yet. The Thin White Duke, lofty, Aryan ('making sure white stains'), was a projection of Bowie's own deluded attachment to the magical symbols of the Far Right. There's a glacial, yearning quality to the music, from the epic title track through to the breathless interpretation of Dimitri Tiomkin's 'Wild Is The Wind'. 'Station To Station' is a rivetingly emotional album but it's the emotion of an individual who has become desperately and spiritually bankrupt.

Recording began in October 1975 at the Cherokee Studios in Hollywood, and again Bowie wrote most of the album in the studio. Bowie was living reversed hours, sleeping during the day and recording through the night, putting his band through the mill in the process.

Finally re-titled 'Station To Station' and released early in 1976 it proved to be a bigger commercial success in America than in Europe. That said, musically it was beginning to move away from the 'plastic soul' of its predecessor towards a more European sound, as evidenced on the Kraftwerk-inspired motorik of the title track. An immensely rich listening experience, this shows Bowie at his very best, although he was reportedly unhappy about the original sound mix. Earl Slick once again takes the role of soloist, and the rhythm section of Alomar, Murray and Davies conjures up an intriguing mélange of 'black' and 'white' styles. Harry Maslin, who had engineered the 'Young Americans' sessions, was brought in as producer.

The cover, a shot from *The Man Who Fell To Earth*, has also now been restored to full colour. It was always the intention to go with a colour photo until Bowie, then planning the 'White Light' 1976 tour, opted for an uncharacteristically bland black and white version instead. The re-issue also contains two live tracks as a bonus. An essential purchase.

STATION TO STATION

This is one of Bowie's best ever. It starts with a synthesised train sound rebounding from speaker to speaker, an obvious nod towards Kraftwerk's 'Autobahn', (the German technocrats were later to repay the compliment with the 'Station To Station'-inspired 'Trans Europe Express'), and, through a hypnotic and gradually intensifying rhythmic figure, builds dramatically towards Bowie's entrance: 'The Return of the Thin White Duke/Throwing darts in lovers' eyes'. The imagery is redolent with Crowleyesque references to magical transformations, and his vocal is ominously multi-tracked. Then suddenly, mid-way through, the piece turns round on itself and, after the killer lines 'It's not the side effects of the cocaine/I'm thinking that it must be love', rocks out passionately until Slick's solo closes the proceedings. An ambitious and awesomely realised piece of music.

GOLDEN YEARS

It was rumoured that this was originally offered to, and discarded by, no less than the Hamburger King of Schmaltz himself, Elvis Presley. Whatever, this is a terrific single, and there are hints of Presleyesque melodrama in the vocal. It's Bowie's best dance track from the Seventies and its insistent riff, cool castanets and catchy refrain are worth the price of the CD alone. 'Golden Years' became a transatlantic Top 10 hit early in 1976.

WORD ON A WING

Those who cringed at Bowie during 'The Lord's Prayer' incident at the Concert For Aids Awareness in 1992, may have deemed his Clifftastic conversion to Christianity a touch odd after the positively Bacchanalian excesses of yore. However, around the time of 'Station To Station', he began wearing a cross as a form of talismanic protection, and this quite beautiful song is no less than a hymn. Roy Bittan is at hand with some delicious piano and the result is a plea for salvation in the midst of Hollywood's excesses.

TVC15

Showing Bowie in lighter vein, this is your average run-of-the-mill song about a girlfriend-eating television set! Influenced by the Thomas Newton figure in *The Man Who Fell To Earth*, who overdosed on the cathode ray in front of a bank of television screens (a trick later famously, and brilliantly, ripped off by U2 in the 1990's), Bowie offers up one of his simplest, and best, hooks: 'Transmission/ Transition', and the band, complete with honky-tonk piano and doo-wop backing vocals, are in jaunty mood. The second single from the album, it stalled in the UK at Number 33, despite being released to coincide with the European leg of the world tour.

STAY

Some of the best guitar work of any Bowie album can be found on this cool cut about the uncertainties of a one-nighter: 'Cos you can never really tell/When somebody wants something you want too'. Always a live favourite of Bowie's, this version has drama a-plenty and remains one of his strongest cuts from the Seventies.

WILD IS THE WIND

(TIOMKIN/WASHINGTON)

Originally recorded by Johnny Mathis in 1956 for the film of the same name, Bowie makes this epic tale of passion his own with a remarkable, highly-mannered vocal performance. The song, driven by some almost aggressive acoustic guitar, twists and turns to full dramatic effect, before falling silent as Bowie croons: 'Don't you know you're life itself'. The song then burns out in one of the most stirring and erotic endings to any pop ballad.

BONUS TRACKS ON 1991 RE-ISSUE:

WORD ON A WING (LIVE) & STAY (LIVE)

The CD re-issue contains these two interesting live versions recorded at the Nassau Coliseum, Long Island, USA on 23 March 1976.

DAVIDBOWIE
LOW

LOW

(ORIGINAL UK ISSUE: RCA VICTOR PL 12030, RELEASED 14 JANUARY 1977; UK CD: EMI EMD 1027; US CD: RYKODISC RCD 10142; UK CHART: 2 [TOTAL WEEKS IN CHART: 24]; US CHART: 11 {7})

1976 was a crisis year for Bowie. Crippled by cocaine, he haunted the stage during a five-month world tour. Off-stage he faced a concerted media backlash in the wake of his alleged Nazi salute at Victoria Station, and some perversely inappropriate (given the rise in Britain of the far-right organisations such as the British Movement and the National Front) observations about Hitler and the need for a new right-wing government to seize the reins of power. In the eyes of many, despite the excellence of his recent recordings, Bowie had flagrantly abused his position as a star.

'Low' – originally entitled 'New Music, Night And Day' – can be seen as an attempt to retreat from the excesses and pressures of this very stardom. At a time when punk rock was noisily reclaiming the three-minute pop song in a show of public defiance, Bowie almost completely abandoned traditional rock instrumentation and embarked on a kind of introverted musical therapy. Recording at the Château d'Herouville studio near Paris and at the Hansa studios in Berlin during the autumn of 1976, he enlisted the help of ex-Roxy Music's Brian Eno and once again recalled Tony Visconti as producer.

Brian Eno remembers: "What I think he was trying to do was to duck the momentum of a successful career. The main problem with success is that it's a huge momentum. It's like you've got this big train behind you and it all wants you to carry on going the same way. Nobody wants you to step off the tracks and start looking round in the scrub around the edges because nobody can see anything promising there."

One of the most unusual features of the recording process was the use of Eno's Oblique Strategies cards which he had developed with Peter Schmidt in 1975. They formed a sort of musical tarot ('over one hundred musical dilemmas' according to the author) and contained directives on how to work in the studio such as 'Listen to the quiet voice', 'Fill every beat with something', 'Emphasize the flaws', 'Mute and continue' and 'Use an unacceptable colour'. Eno urged Bowie to experiment and to think in non-linear ways about the recording process, and he went on to develop this new approach throughout the rest of the decade.

For Bowie fans the resulting album could hardly have been more challenging. He had completely abandoned narrative structures in his songs. The 'songs' which form the first side of the album sound like mere fragments or half-reported conversations. Side 2, comprising four long instrumental tracks, reportedly gave RCA a collective coronary and led one executive to suggest to Bowie that he might relocate back to Los Angeles and record more 'Young Americans'-style hit material. Bowie, however, had the last laugh: 'Sound And Vision', the album's first single, reached Number 3 in the UK charts.

'Low', never a big seller, remains an uncompromising work, and it is more talked about and admired than actually liked or listened to, except by Bowie die-hards and rock critics. Its snob value was confirmed when Philip Glass resurrected three tracks ('Warszawa', 'Subterraneans' and 'Some Are') for his puzzlingly jaunty neo-Romantic Low Symphony (Point Music 438 150 2) in 1993. 'Low''s significance in the general scheme of things cannot, however, be overestimated and it stands not only as Bowie's most innovative work to date, but as a landmark in popular music history. Its prescient use of ambient musical structures and Bowie's blanked-out, expressionless vocals influenced a whole generation of British post-punk artists from Joy Division to Gary Numan. Perhaps more importantly, just as punk was helping to democratise the guitar, Bowie and Eno, along with Germany's Kraftwerk, were making the synthesiser cool and poppy after a decade of Emerson Lake and Palmer and pseudo-classical meanderings.

'Low' was re-released on CD in 1991, reaching Number 64 in the UK charts. It contained three bonus tracks, 'Some Are', 'All Saints' and a remix of 'Sound And Vision'. Incidentally, the cover artwork, based on a still from *The Man Who Fell To Earth* which shows a duffle-coated Bowie in profile, was intended as a punning statement on Bowie's new solitude – his Low profile! Hardly corset-snapping humour to be sure, but not bad from someone who only a year before had been storing his urine in a refrigerator. Allegedly.

SPEED OF LIFE

Bowie's instrumental opener immediately sets the tone for the first half of the album: treated synthesiser figures, a crashing distorted snare-drum and some highly unusual melody lines (this time faintly reminiscent of the very elderly 'Whispering' recorded in 1922 by Paul Whiteman). All in all, one of Bowie's most successful instrumental tracks. The wonderfully spacey descending synth line was, of course, resurrected three years later for 'Scary Monsters'.

BREAKING GLASS

(BOWIE, DAVIS, MURRAY)

Clocking in at just 1 minute 42 this song fragment shows the direct influence of Eno. Rather than ask Bowie to flesh out the song with an extra verse, Eno again opted for the 'if it's not broken don't fix it' method and the result is a song which is perfectly half-formed. The lyrics in themselves don't really matter: what makes the song is Bowie's coked-out delivery, a winning guitar line and that clever three-note synth swoop from speaker to speaker.

WHAT IN THE WORLD

The weakest song in the set, it's neither sufficiently weird nor melodically telling, and Bowie is buried beneath a discordant art rock backing. Lyrically it continues the themes of alienation and claustrophobic introspection which infuse the album: 'So deep in your room/You never leave your room', but 'Sound And Vision' does it much better. Unaccountably, the song was a live favourite of Bowie's and featured on the 1978 tour, the Serious Moonlight comeback tour in 1983 and on some dates on the 'Outside' tour in 1995/96.

SOUND AND VISION

The crashing metronomic instrumental opening of 'Sound And Vision', together with Mary Visconti's (née Hopkins) backing vocals and cribbed synthesised Mantovani-style strings presumably became a favourite of the Director General of the BBC as it was used throughout the early part of 1977 as background music for continuity announcements. RCA must have been glad of this exposure as Bowie himself did nothing to promote it. It's justifiably one of Bowie's greatest singles. You can dance to it, marvel at Bowie's cyborg croon and enshroud yourself in its melancholic grandeur: 'Blue, blue electric blue/that's the colour of my room/Where I will live'. Bowie's ultimate retreat song.

ALWAYS CRASHING IN THE SAME CAR

Two resounding successes on 'Low' are Dennis

Davis' drumming and Tony Visconti's treatment of the snare drum using a gadget called the 'harmoniser', which created a drop in pitch. 'Always Crashing In The Same Car' utilises this effect to the full and Bowie adds some suitably violent images to go along with the stark musical backdrop.

BE MY WIFE

The second single off the album and, despite a promo featuring a frighteningly contrived performance by a hammy Bowie in full flow, a complete flop. It's another fine track, perhaps the most conventional in terms of song structure on the album, with a memorable honky-tonk piano opening, great riff courtesy of Ricky Gardener and the album's most direct lyric 'Please be mine/Share my life/Stay with me/Be my wife'. The song was dusted down as one of Bowie's own choices for the phone-your-fave Sound + Vision tour of 1990.

A NEW CAREER IN A NEW TOWN

A second short instrumental closes the vinyl Side two. The track is an incongruous mix of the cool, alienating timbres of the synthesiser overlaid with Bowie's harmonica. The result is a kind of battle between the European (specifically German) tradition of calculated metronomic synth music and the wholesome authenticity of the Yankee harmonica. Intriguing.

WARSZAWA

(BOWIE/ENO)

This bleak, funereally slow instrumental was an attempt by Bowie to capture the textures of the Polish countryside in general, and the city of Warsaw in particular. Midway into the instrumental Bowie booms out in what sounds like a real language (but isn't) and the result is as far away from the mainstream as he has ever got. The use of phonetically constructed 'none-sense' in popular culture wasn't new (the Dadaists had evolved something called 'Sound Poetry' in the 1910s), but Bowie pioneered its resurgence, as the career of the post-Punk British indie-darlings The Cocteau Twins proved.

ART DECADE

Bowie said that here he was trying to capture the ambience of West Berlin, 'cut off from the world, art and culture, dying with no hope of retribution'. Another slow instrumental utilising a variety of synths, piano and cello, it still sounds stark and unnerving two decades on.

WEEPING WALL

Philip Glass's neo-classical accumulative work, in which the process of music-making is as important as the end result, is an obvious influence on this instrumental track, which again takes Berlin as its subject-matter. Bowie plays all instruments and sets the shiny but 'real' timbres of the xylophone and vibraphone against the synths.

SUBTERRANEANS

This track, or an earlier version of it, was originally demoed for the never-completed Bowie soundtrack to *The Man Who Fell To Earth*. It completes the trilogy of instrumentals about Berlin, this time dealing with the East. Bowie later commented that it was 'about the people who got caught up in East Berlin after separation – hence the faint jazz saxophones representing the memory of what it was'.

BONUS TRACKS ON 1991 RE-ISSUE:

SOME ARE

(BOWIE/ ENO)

On 'Low' Bowie was able better than ever before to give expression to concepts difficult to articulate in words. Texture comes to dominate over lyrical content, often with telling results. This song is a perfect example: his vocal is high in the mix, yet the words are mainly incomprehensible, breathed out against a haunting piano line with what sounds like the chatter of a half-remembered schoolyard as ambient material.

ALL SAINTS

(BOWIE/ENO)

Another short instrumental and well worth inclusion as a bonus track. Bowie and Eno construct an aboriginal sci-fi apocalypse with synthesisers! Sounds impossible, but it works wonderfully with the synth aping a didgeridoo.

SOUND AND VISION

Poppy 1991 remix with an added saxophone line, vastly inferior to the original. Its inclusion at the end of this most introspective and uncertain of recordings is incongruously jaunty and off-putting. Incidentally, more successful remixes of the track can be found on the 808 State versus David Bowie Maxi CD (Tommy Boy/Rykodisc TB CD 510).

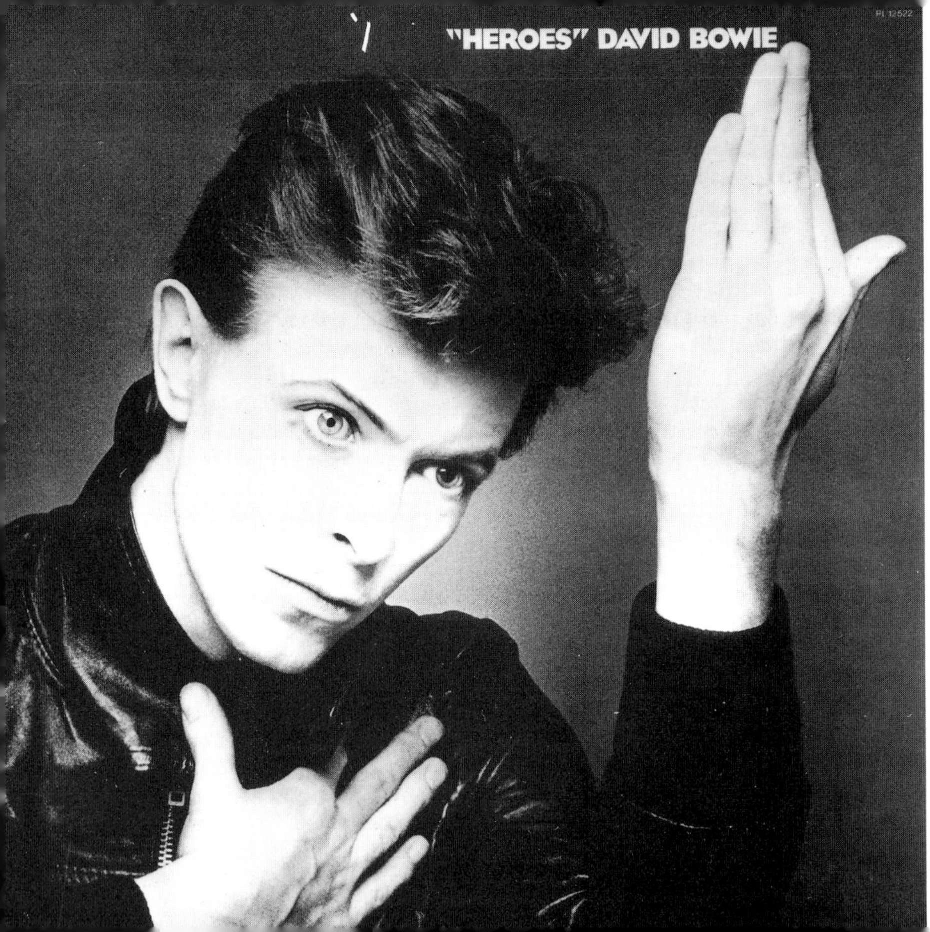
PL 12522
"HEROES" DAVID BOWIE

"HEROES"

(ORIGINAL UK ISSUE: RCA VICTOR PL 12522, RELEASED 14 OCTOBER 1977; UK CD: EMI EMD 1025; US CD: RYKODISC RCD 10143; UK CHART: 3 [TOTAL WEEKS IN CHART: 26]; US CHART: 35 [3])

In a famous advertising legend for the "Heroes" album, RCA proclaimed 'There's Old Wave, there's New Wave and there's David Bowie'. In the year that the angry sloganising of punk dominated the press, Bowie and Eno offered two albums which showed another, more private, musical world and which would arguably go on to have just as great an influence as any Sex Pistols record.

"Heroes", like its predecessor 'Low', was recorded with largely the same personnel during the summer of 1977 at the Hansa Studios in Berlin. Robert Fripp, then ex-King Crimson, was brought in by Eno as lead guitarist and his contribution made for some stirring moments. Eno knew that Fripp would respond best by being surprised into action: "We put the songs on. These were songs he'd never heard... He didn't know what the chords were going to do, what the changes were going to be... He would just launch into them at full speed and somehow navigate his way through them."

However, the key to "Heroes"' decadent grandeur was its site of production. The studio's control room, which housed the producer's console, was overlooked by armed soldiers in an observation tower on the Wall only a matter of yards away. This, as Eno was later to comment, was an environment which forced them into some sort of greatness: blandness would have been totally inappropriate as an end result. The album was completed extremely quickly, taking only a month to write and record, and many of the takes used were first ones. Whereas 'Low' is the better record, it was "Heroes" which won the plaudits at the time, becoming *Melody Maker*'s Album of the Year.

With "Heroes" he retreats even further from the role of rock icon: "I feel incredibly divorced from rock and it's a genuine striving to be that way," he told *Melody Maker* soon after the album's release. "Heroes" has a cinematic quality, with the instrumental section, found originally on Side 2 of the album, overshadowing what is, in truth, a rather weak set of more conventional songs on Side 1. The six-minute title track dominates four lesser vignettes.

"Heroes" has also been portrayed as a more emotional and positive album than its predecessor, but there is actually very little evidence of Bowie lightening up. The mood remains sombre, often brilliantly so. His music was also becoming truly international in its scope (a trend further emphasised on the last in the Bowie-Eno tryptich, 'Lodger') and was beginning to incorporate non-Western musical motifs. By the end of 1977 Bowie had reaffirmed his position as Britain's most innovative artist.

BEAUTY AND THE BEAST

This discordant song, with a trademark repetitious riff, is not the strongest of opening cuts and reached a lowly Number 39 in the UK charts when released as a single in early 1978.

JOE THE LION

The album only really kicks into gear with this tale of performance artist Chris Burden. Burden liked being put in a bag on a motorway, being hung over a pool of water with two electrodes in his hand, and, yes, being nailed to his car. It was this idea of ritual performance art, of the body-as-art-object, that informs much of the writing on the 'Outside' album eighteen years later. According to Bowie, Fripp's idiosyncratic guitar playing was his attempt at the blues, and Bowie's half-spoken middle section and scream – 'You will be like your dreams tonight' – is one of the album's best moments.

"HEROES"

(BOWIE/ENO)

In "Heroes" Bowie gives the impression that you can be like your dreams forever. This is the only piece of narrative writing on the album and is perhaps pop's definitive statement of the potential triumph of the human spirit over adversity. It is also a classic example of how music, lyrics and context must always be brought into equivalence when assessing a song's impact, as this particular song is nothing without Fripp's guitar work and the slowly building ominously repetitive musical refrain which builds into an almost excruciating climax. Visconti claims that the lovers' secret rendezvous by the Berlin Wall depicted in the song actually refers to an affair he was having during the recording process. Whatever, it's gone down as one of Bowie's most famous songs, undoubtedly due to a succession of high-profile live renditions (notably at Live Aid) which have tended to obscure the irony intended by the quotation marks of the original. Released in an unsatisfactorily edited form as a single in the autumn of 1977 it only reached Number 24 in the UK charts.

SONS OF THE SILENT AGE

Here Bowie serves up a slice of nostalgic futurism, as if we've been transported to some time centuries hence and are listening to a re-telling of the story of a long-gone era. Again, it's the incongruity of the structure of the song which is of interest, with its doomy, leaden, sax-driven verses and almost schmaltzy choruses.

BLACKOUT

There was some speculation amongst Bowie fans at the time that this song referred to Bowie's own collapse (sensationally reported as a heart attack) in 1976, but this has been denied by the man himself. It's another lyrical and musical cut-up *à la* 'Beauty And The Beast', but this time Bowie's vocals have a breathless, haughty manner ('Me I'm Robin Hood and I puff on my cigarette') and there's some great drumming from Dennis Davies.

V-2 SCHNEIDER

After a set of more conventional songs which only show Bowie on half-power, the album really releases its charms with the four instrumental pieces. This is probably the best of the lot, as Bowie leads the band through a goose-stepping piece of music with an off-the-beat sax part (Bowie had begun his part on the wrong beat but decided to keep it like that), some effective military-style drumming and great guitars.

SENSE OF DOUBT

This is a good example of how Bowie and Eno were able to build up the expressive quality of their music using what is in essence a very simple piece of musical information. As notes on a page there's very little going on with this track, but the main four-note descending refrain has such awesome resonance and the high synth line is so disturbing and funereal that the result is a minimalist masterpiece.

This track appeared as the B-side of the 'Beauty And The Beast' single and, as such, found its way on to a few pub juke-boxes. Bowie fans with a droll sense of humour liked nothing better than to observe its effects on a cheerful crowd of drinkers.

MOSS GARDEN

(BOWIE/ENO)

From funereal to ethereal on this highly effective, slowly moving piece of music. It's obviously meant to carry Japanese musical connotations and Bowie's koto (a stringed instrument similar to the guitar) works well. Eno's influence is felt everywhere on this track, as the musical structures change almost imperceptibly. In the Eighties and Nineties Eno's video installations would visually re-create the minimalism of his Seventies music with their slowly changing image collages.

NEUKÖLN

(BOWIE/ENO)

'Moss Garden' segues straight into this instrumental. The Zen tranquillity is disrupted by, again, some fine guitar work (again with a five-note descending riff) and Bowie's asthmatic melismatic sax. By the end of the piece the sax is alone and Bowie booms out like a ship in a fog-bound harbour. 'Neuköln', by the way, is an area in the former East Berlin populated in the main by Turkish immigrants.

THE SECRET LIFE OF ARABIA

(BOWIE/ENO/ALOMAR)

This vocal track has tended to be ignored, which is a shame as, along with the title track, it's the album's best song. There's an infectious groove which builds and builds in a typically Bowiesque repetitious manner and Bowie once again returns to the camp theme of real life being merely a bit-part acting role: 'You must see the movie/The sand in my eyes/I walk through a desert song/When the heroine dies'.

BONUS TRACKS ON 1991 RE-ISSUE:

ABDULMAJID

The middle-Eastern theme is neatly continued with the addition of this instrumental track, which again is hauntingly repetitious. Well worth being included and, for once, it doesn't upset the plot of the original album too much.

JOE THE LION (1991 RE-MIX)

An almost identical, and therefore superfluous, re-mix of the second track.

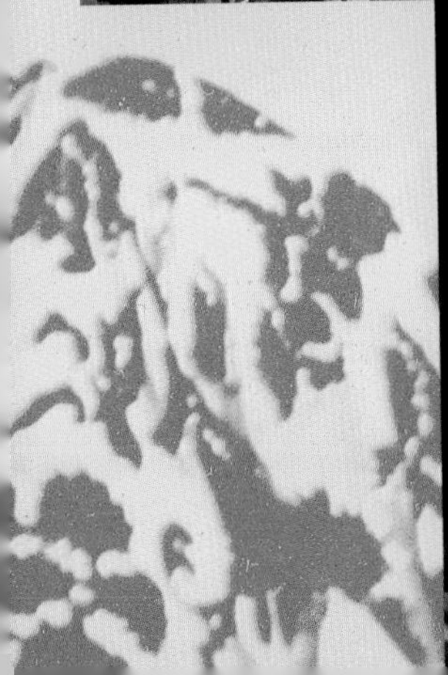

STAGE

(ORIGINAL UK ISSUE: RCA VICTOR PL 02913, RELEASED 25 SEPTEMBER 1978; UK CD: EMI EMD 1030; US CD: RYKODISC RCD 10144/45; UK CHART: 5 [TOTAL WEEKS IN CHART: 10] US CHART: 35)

The Euro-funk of the 1976 Thin White Duke tour yielded a number of high quality bootleg recordings but this, recorded at the Spectrum Arena, Philadelphia on 29 April 1978, although interesting, is rather less essential.

'Stage' producer Visconti played around with the tour's running order and organised the songs chronologically, thus destroying any dramatic impact the show might have had. He also mixed the album so as to make the material sound as much like their originals as possible and, taken together with a very low audience level, it makes for a sterile listening experience. The recent 'Low' and 'Heroes' cuts have warmer, less-forbidding timbres, and

'Breaking Glass', unsuccessfully extended into a more formal rock song, was put out on an EP with 'Ziggy Stardust' and 'Art Decade', which reached Number 54 in the UK charts.

The Ziggy-era material, however, is interesting, with Adrian Belew's guitar mixing fluently with Simon House's violin, and Bowie sings wonderfully well on a version of 'Heroes' which, like the German language version he also recorded, is better than the original. That and a great version of 'Fame' aside, this is for Bowiephiles only.

Full track listing, Disc 1: 'Hang On To Yourself', 'Ziggy Stardust', 'Five Years', 'Soul Love', 'Star', 'Station To Station', 'Fame', 'TVC 15'

Disc 2: 'Warszawa', 'Speed Of Life', 'Art Decade', 'Sense Of Doubt', 'Breaking Glass', 'Heroes', 'What In The World', 'Blackout', 'Beauty And The Beast', 'Alabama Song' (bonus track on 1991 CD re-issue).

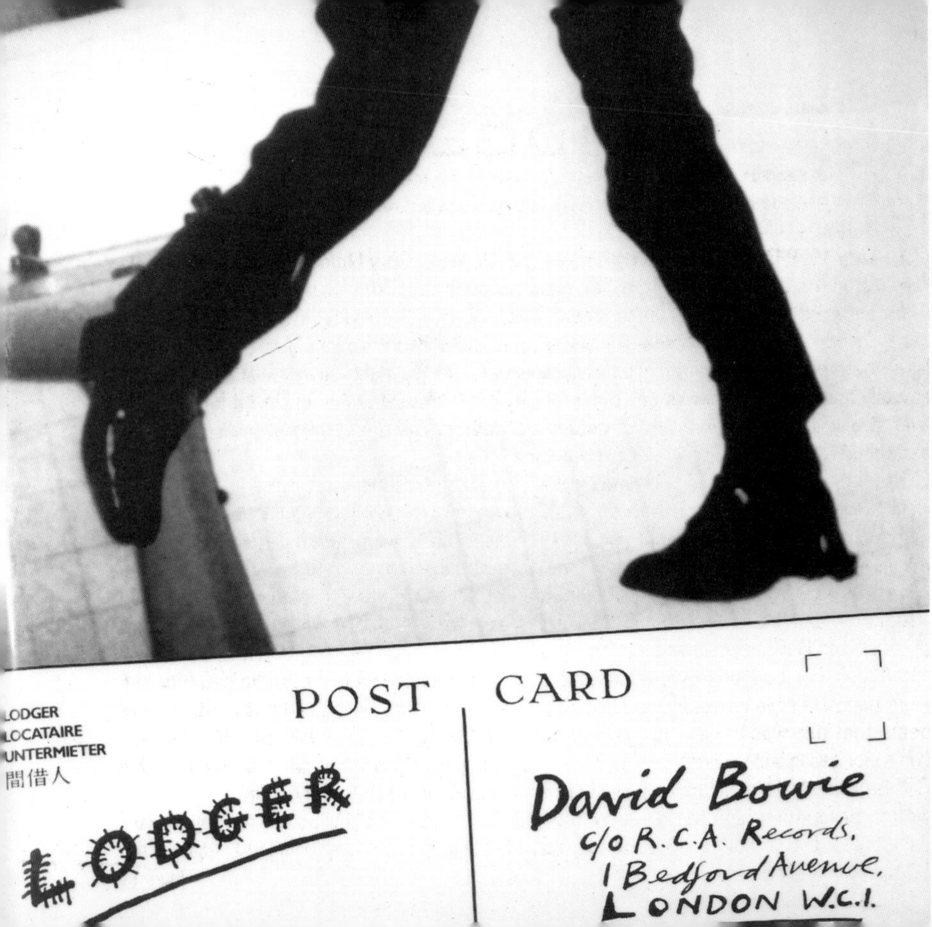
POST CARD
LODGER
LOCATAIRE
UNTERMIETER
間借人
LODGER
David Bowie
c/o R.C.A. Records,
1 Bedford Avenue,
LONDON W.C.1.

LODGER

(ORIGINAL UK ISSUE: RCA BOW LP 1, RELEASED 18 MAY 1979; UK CD: EMI EMD 1026, US CD: RYKODISC RCD 10146; UK CHART: 4 [TOTAL WEEKS IN CHART: 17]; US CHART: 20 [8])

By early 1979 Bowie was finding himself 'out-Bowied'. Gary Numan, a failed punk-rocker turned robotic androgyny, with a head full of Bowie, Ultravox and Kraftwerk, proved to be an unexpected mainstream success when his band Tubeway Army hit Number 1 in the UK with 'Are Friends Electric?' Numan was suitably other-worldly and, for a time at least, before he started droning on about aviation and the righteousness of Thatcherism, actually made great, under-valued pop records. In the absence of a big UK hit for Bowie in over two years, it looked as if his natural constituency of the emotionally dispossessed had opted for an ersatz version of the real thing.

The 'Lodger' album, which hit the shops just as Numan-mania was breaking out, was a demanding affair. Recorded during a gap in the 1978 world tour and completed in early 1979, (its working titles included 'Planned Accidents' and 'Despite Straight Lines') it revealed the Bowie-Eno collaboration in its final throes. For 'Lodger' Bowie returned to a more narrative style of writing, and one suspects that this was beginning to grate on Eno's pioneering ambient stance.

This collision of styles (the rock idol beginning to grasp for mainstream acceptance once again, the pop pioneer deepening his interest in ambient structures) makes for an uneasy, though often brilliant musical trip. The album has unjustly suffered in the eyes of posterity, not least due to Eno's constant dismissal of it in a succession of interviews. Its main flaw is that its sound is 'graced' with one of the most demanding mixes of any Bowie record. Unless it is played on superior hi-fi equipment the vinyl 'Lodger' sounds unclear and soupy, the top end dulled, while the bass lacks any resonance. On CD the sound is much improved but still not great.

Although the album boasts the trans-sexual hit single 'Boys Keep Swinging', eclecticism and experimentation have lessened its mainstream appeal. A pity since much of 'Lodger' is really exciting and the use of ethnic musics on Side 1 extremely prescient. 'Lodger' is loosely thematic, with the first half commenting on Bowie's wanderlust and the second on Anglo-American consumer society. An underrated work, it's there for anyone interested in Bowie's more daring musical legacy. And the cover, in the form of a postcard and showing Bowie on the mortuary slab with nose and legs squashed at right-angles, is one of his most innovatory.

FANTASTIC VOYAGE

(BOWIE, ENO)

After the jagged, ominous music of 'Heroes', Lodger starts off with a surprisingly delicate, mandolin-led ballad which harks back to the narrative styles of 'Hunky Dory'. It also indicates the beginnings of a certain politicisation in Bowie's work, dealing as it does with the threat of the holocaust and the 'depression' of our leaders. Incidentally, the song has exactly the same chord sequence as 'Boys Keep Swinging'.

AFRICAN NIGHT FLIGHT

(BOWIE, ENO)

This is the most innovatory piece of music on the album. Suitably jungle-like noises abound, and the musical fabric is dense with Eno's synthesised 'cricket menace'. Bowie's vocal delivery, as he was later to comment, is a sort of white rap delivered at break-neck speed and is extremely eccentric, the whole giving the impression of great velocity. The listener feels as if she is being dragged through the undergrowth along with a babbling Bowie. Narratively, the 'song' deals with some German fighter pilots Bowie had met in the bars of Mombasa who felt so culturally alienated that they couldn't return home. More Man Who Fell To Earthisms.

MOVE ON

Another unusually intense ballad, this time with a melody far superior to 'Fantastic Voyage'. Thematically it's the key-note song on the first half of the album. Here he is 'just a travelling man' and in a typically corny moment Bowie croons 'Cyprus is my Island/When the going's rough/I would like to find you/Somewhere in a place like that'.

YASSASSIN

Fine vocal phrasing is the feature of this catchy, Middle-Eastern 'Fame' re-write, which was surprisingly left as an album cut only. Bowie sings 'We walked proud and lustful/In this resonant world' and stretches the first syllable of 'resonant' over five notes, imbuing the line with an appropriate melismatic quality. Simon House's violin is pretty good too. ('Yassassin' is Turkish for 'long life')

RED SAILS

(BOWIE, ENO)

In which Bowie gambles on a piece of ambient-pop sounding good on your average hi-fi equipped with a darning needle as a stylus. I'll let Bowie try and explain what's going on here: "Here we took a German new music feel and put against it the idea of a contemporary English mercenary-cum-swashbuckling Errol Flynn, and put him in the China Sea. We have a lovely cross-reference of cultures. I honestly don't know what it's about". The ending, in particular, is one of my favourites, with Bowie yelling 'The hinterland, the hinterland/ We're going to sail to the hinterland'. Barmy.

D.J.

(BOWIE, ENO, ALOMAR)

There's a marked shift in focus now, as Bowie abandons his Marco Polo, roving pop-God act. 'DJ' is a good song, but, even in an edited form, proved too tangled structurally for the singles charts, peaking at its début position of 29 in the UK. Again, the use of violin works well and Bowie's in great 'amateur operatics' form vocally, but you need to see the video too for the song to really take off.

LOOK BACK IN ANGER

(BOWIE/ENO)

This song, about a rather seedy angel of death and possessor of a fabulous video, never actually became a single in the UK. A pity since it's one of the album's most dramatic moments, with a great droning quality, and fine guitar break in the middle. It proved a worthy opener to many of the Serious Moonlight concerts four years later and was revived on the 1995 Outside tour.

BOYS KEEP SWINGING

(BOWIE/ENO)

Bowie famously instructed the band to swap

instruments in order to get a raw, garage rock sound, and the closing guitar solo at the end of the track is fanatically awkward and discordant. Released as the lead-off•single it reached Number 7 in the UK charts but deserved much better. Lyrically, Bowie has rather cheekily rewritten The Village People's 'In The Navy' for this tale of hetero/homo-sexual laddishness: 'When you're a boy/You can wear a uniform/When you're a boy/Other boys check you out'. Who could forget Bowie being chased around the studio by Kenny Everett as 'Angry of Mayfair' screamed 'I fought in the war for the likes of you. And I never got one!' on *The Kenny Everett Video Show*? Well, I certainly haven't, and as for that video...

REPETITION

In this most alarming piece of descriptive writing Bowie tells a tale of wife-beating and marital disharmony in a mundane, matter-of-fact way. The metronomic guitar riff mirrors perfectly the repeated blows dished out by husband to wife. An undervalued song and one of his best.

RED MONEY

(BOWIE/ALOMAR)

Here Bowie commandeers the music of Iggy Pop's great 'Sister Midnight' (actually performed by Bowie on his 1976 tour) and sets against it some observations on consumer society and the responsibility money brings. A surprisingly flat ending to a fine album.

BONUS TRACKS ON 1991 RE-ISSUE:

I PRAY, OLÉ

This is a great cut, guitars and violins intermesh forming another typically dense structure, and Bowie's insistent vocal 'Can you make, can you make it through' make this a bonus track well worth the listen.

LOOK BACK IN ANGER

(BOWIE/ENO)

This is a 1988 re-recording of the track which formed the basis of Bowie's live performance at the ICA that year starring Reeves Gabrels on guitar. An interesting re-working.

David Bowie
Scary

SCARY MONSTERS (AND SUPERCREEPS)

(ORIGINAL UK ISSUE: RCA BOW LP 2, RELEASED 12 SEPTEMBER 1980; US CD: RYKODISC RCD 20147; UK CHART: 1 [TOTAL WEEKS IN CHART: 32]; US CHART: 12 [11])

For many Bowie fans, the release of 'Scary Monsters (and Supercreeps)' in the autumn of 1980 marked the end of a golden era. It was the last album to feature the production skills of Tony Visconti and the rhythm section of George Murray, Dennis Davis and Carlos Alomar (though the last named has worked with Bowie on subsequent projects). Although booked to produce the 'Let's Dance' album late in 1982, Visconti was dropped at the last minute in favour of Nile Rodgers, and the last time he worked with Bowie was during the UK leg of the Serious Moonlight tour in 1983 when he was asked to sort out the sound mix for the Edinburgh and Hammersmith shows. Visconti claims that the rift was caused by certain comments to Bowie biographers which were perceived as disloyal by Bowie. Bowie claims Visconti talked too much to the media about his son Joe. Whatever, his absence almost certainly contributed to the drop in standard of Bowie's output in the mid-Eighties.

On 'Scary Monsters' Visconti and Bowie, this time without Eno, fashioned what is arguably Bowie's finest record to date. The sound is uncompromising – a huge, cavernous drum sound and some truly manic guitar work from Robert Fripp. These are guitar solos without any of the machismo and predictability which characterises most rock guitar-playing, and they teeter, screech and tear through the songs, far and away the best pieces of guitar work yet on any Bowie album. Indeed, the whole set shows Bowie at the height of his powers: musically he's adroit at pulling off both the wondrous synth swoop of 'Ashes To Ashes', the dementia of 'It's No Game' and the New York-styled funk of 'Fashion'. Lyrically, Bowie plays the role of battered and wearied narrator, in turn both cautionary (as on

'It's No Game', and 'Teenage Wildlife'), and predicatory (as on 'Scream Like A Baby). Vocally the set runs the whole gamut from the 'Newleyesque' cockney of the title track to the burnt-out resignation of 'It's No Game Part II'.

A more dynamic and commercial work than 'Lodger', 'Scary Monsters'' success was founded, however, on one of his strongest ever singles – 'Ashes To Ashes' – which became Bowie's second UK Number 1. With Bowie the packaging has always been as important as the music itself, and in 1980 he hit upon the perfect blend of commerciality and innovation wrapped up in the disguise of a Renaissance clown, a perfect trailblazer for the New Romantics on the horizon. At the time, the mannequin-like Pierrot-Bowie which adorned the covers of both album and single, and which featured in that unforgettable video, looked just like the latest instalment in the continuing cartoonesque trawl throughout the many untapped characters of the Bowie psyche. Little did we know that it was to be the end of an era. Greeted with almost unanimously good reviews at the time (*Record Mirror*'s Simon Ludgate famously awarded it seven out of a maximum of five stars!), 'Scary Monsters' is an essential item.

Bowie never promoted the album live, incidentally, choosing instead to act with some distinction as the crippled John Merrick in stage productions of *The Elephant Man* in Chicago and New York.

IT'S NO GAME (PART 1)

The sound of a vacuum cleaner, the Cobra-like hollow rattle of a castanet and then a lurch straight into this remarkable opening salvo. The dye is cast – a huge ambient snare sound echoes through the mix, and then Bowie tries to out-scream Japanese singer Michi Hirota, who replies to Bowie's lines with a Japanese translation. Bowie said that he wanted to 'break down a particular kind of sexist attitude about women and I thought that the Japanese girl typifies it, where everybody sort of pictures a geisha girl – sweet, demure and non-thinking. So she sang the lyrics in a macho, samurai voice'.

UP THE HILL BACKWARDS

This was the album's fourth, and least successful, single (UK chart Number 32). The lazy, non-committal stance in the lyrics is turned around in a blazing final minute as Robert Fripp's exhilarating guitar figures give the piece a most committed ending.

SCARY MONSTERS (AND SUPERCREEPS)

Fripp's guitar again detonates to wild effect in this tale of a girl who's 'stupid in the streets and can't socialise'. Although at the time Bowie was keen to impress on his public that his drug period was over, songs such as these, redolent as they are with images of paranoia and violence, give a strong hint that drug-induced schizophrenic states were not something he had totally left behind. Indeed, in interviews in the Nineties, Bowie admitted that his association with hard drugs lasted well into the Eighties. The music also has a foreboding, melismatic, Middle-Eastern quality which was later echoed in rock by tracks such as Echo And The Bunnymen's 'The Cutter' in 1983 and the excellent PIL single 'Rise' in 1986. The third single off the album, it reached the UK Top 20 in January 1981.

ASHES TO ASHES

With the addition of some Goons-like frivolity in the instrumental break in the middle, this version is slightly more extended than the single release. A classic pop song, incantatory and multi-layered, this is Bowie recapturing his melodic touch in a huge wash of synthesisers and treated guitars. 'Ashes To Ashes' updates the Major Tom saga from 'Space Oddity' and remains the only sequel to reach Number 1 in the UK Charts. And Bowie got the queasy, Edwardian, nursery rhyme-like quality just right in the sing-along dénouement: 'My mother said/To get things done/you'd better not mess with Major Tom' – a sneaky and sinister re-write of a children's nursery rhyme ('My mummy said/that I never should/play with the Gypsies in the wood').

FASHION

According to Tony Visconti, Bowie had a riff based around the word 'Jamaica' which refused to take the form of a song until the very end of the recording session. That this almost-lost song fragment went on to become one of Bowie's live staples and a sizeable hit (UK Number 5) is testimony to Bowie's quicksilver improvisatory talents and Visconti's production skills. The result is both a jaundiced view of the very musical culture Bowie was using to such good effect, that of dance and disco ('It's loud and it's tasteless and I've heard it before'), and a sly put-down of style fascism – something Bowie could be accused of himself. There's also a great, driving rhythm section and the gloriously arrogant 'Listen to me/Don't listen to me' middle eight.

TEENAGE WILDLIFE

This sprawling, ambitious track has for too long been regarded as a just an inferior 'Heroes' re-write. In fact it's a fine song which lyrically continues 'Fashion's theme of world-wearied, patrician pessimism, with Bowie, then the 33-year-old paternal figure, pronouncing on youth culture from a marked distance. In fact, 'Scary Monsters' reveals a Bowie heading towards an uncertain middle age and commenting on this uncertainty (unlike 'Let's Dance', which seems to revel in maturity and being well-adjusted). The vocal performance on this track is gargantuan and the epic quality of the music makes for an underrated, and often ignored, Bowie classic.

SCREAM LIKE A BABY

This track has a calculated New York, New Wave feel, and is based, musically, on a track Bowie wrote back in 1973 for Ava Cherry's group The Astronettes called 'I Am A Laser', now available on the CD 'People From Bad Homes' (Golden Years, GY005). 'Scream Like A Baby' continues the Bowie tradition of nostalgic science fiction. This time Bowie, as narrator, re-tells a futuristic tale of incarceration and sexual persecution in a distant past. The best moment comes towards the end of the track when Bowie, through the use of two vari-speed vocals, brilliantly captures the sense of a mind being split in two and the sort of schizophrenic horror which had troubled him in real life through much of his career as a singer.

KINGDOM COME

(VERLAINE)

This Tom Verlaine song roots the album's creative spiritual home in the late-Seventies American post-punk scene and as a homage works well. The highlight is of course the astonishingly contrived vocal performance in which Bowie attempts an almost psychotic Barry Gibb-like phrasing.

BECAUSE YOU'RE YOUNG

This, the weakest song in the set, would still

have cruised on to the set-list of any of the subsequent Bowie recordings in the Eighties. Pete Townshend lends some characteristically springy, jagged guitar, but the theme of past master commenting on the trifles of youth is now overplayed and Bowie's overblown vocal finale can't rescue it.

Bowie later commented on how surprised he was to note that, in the studio, Townshend played with the same athleticism he brought to his stage performances, jumping around and even spinning his right arm while playing.

IT'S NO GAME (PART 2)

The vinyl version ended with this re-working of the opening track. Both band and singer sound exhausted after the sonic bruising they've just administered, and the line 'Put a bullet in my brain and it makes all the papers' with hindsight proved a gruesome prediction for a famous friend. In early December Radio 1's Andy Peebles went out to interview Bowie about his new album and recent theatre triumph in *The Elephant Man* on Broadway. Peebles unexpectedly also caught up with John Lennon and found him in optimistic mood and talking of a future tour. Two days later he was shot dead. What the full effect of the murder of a good musician friend had on Bowie is hard to tell. However, his disappearance from the music scene for two-and-a-half years and his re-launch as a pop idol without the schizoid and obsessive trappings of old might just have been a response to the ultimate example of fan-worship taken too far.

BONUS TRACKS ON 1991 RE-ISSUE:

SPACE ODDITY

On New Year's Eve 1979, Bowie appeared simultaneously in Britain and America, bidding farewell to what many critics point out as being his decade. In America, Bowie performed on Saturday Night Live with Klaus Nomi, dressed in a full-length skirt for 'TVC 15'. In Britain he was featured on *The Kenny Everett Video Show* performing this stark, stripped down acoustic version of many people's favourite Bowie-oldie. An interesting and worthwhile bonus track, it's hard not to see this as an attempt to re-create the Lennon sound of songs such as 'Remember' from his Plastic Ono Band album of 1970.

PANIC IN DETROIT

This re-recording of the 'Aladdin Sane' track is inferior to the original and of interest to Bowie completists only.

CRYSTAL JAPAN

This pleasant, though hardly essential, instrumental track was originally recorded for a Japanese Saki advert which featured The Thin White Duke himself, and could previously have been found on the flip side of the 'Up The Hill Backwards' single.

ALABAMA SONG

This is a studio version of a 1930 Kurt Weill / Bertolt Brecht song which featured prominently in the 1978 world tour and would get an occasional airing on the 1990 Sound + Vision outing. Recorded in Montreux in 1978, it was released as a single in 1980 and surprisingly reached as high as Number 23 in the UK Charts, backed by the re-recorded version of 'Space Oddity' in early 1980. Bowie is in fine thespian fettle, though it will hardly appeal to the casual fan.

DAVID
BOWIE
L E T S
D A N C E

LET'S DANCE

(ORIGINAL UK ISSUE: EMI AMERICA AML 3029, RELEASED 14 APRIL 1983 ; UK CD: EMI CDP 7 46002 2, RE-ISSUED 31 OCTOBER 1995 VIRGIN AMERICA AND 13 NOVEMBER 1995 VIRGIN EUROPE; UK CHART: 1 [TOTAL WEEKS IN CHART: 56]; US CHART: 4 [34])

1983 was the biggest year yet for David Bowie. In January he finally split from RCA and signed for EMI America in a deal reputedly worth 17 million dollars. In the spring his new single 'Let's Dance' became a transatlantic Number 1 and the album of the same name became his biggest-selling album to date. On July 16 Bowie had a staggering ten albums in the UK Top 100 album chart, as throngs of new admirers snapped up his illustrious back catalogue which had just been re-released by RCA at a special-offer price. For the rest of 1983 Bowie's Serious Moonlight tour broke box-office records round the world as his suave, svelte, son-of-Sinatra routine worked a treat.

What was the key to this memorable comeback? Firstly, the album itself hit all the right response buttons. Although its predecessor 'Scary Monsters' had been brilliant, it was still too awkward for mainstream consumption in the States. 'Let's Dance' was warm, humanistic and funky and, 'Ricochet' apart, overtly commercial. Co-produced by Chic's Nile Rodgers it positively swung along, driven by a great honking sax section and some genuinely bluesy guitar from the late Stevie Ray Vaughn.

It was also five years since the last Bowie tour, and almost three since his last studio album. The strong showings of some unlikely interim measures such as the collaboration with Queen on 'Under Pressure' in 1981(UK Number 1), and the then five-year-old and totally freaky duet with Bing Crosby on 'Little Drummer Boy/Peace On Earth' (UK Number 3) at Christmas 1992 proved that his commercial stock had never been higher. Since 1980 the unjustly maligned New Romantic movement headed by Visage, Culture Club and Duran Duran had peopled Planet Pop with little David Bowies. The garish narcissism of New Romanticism brought disco and club culture back on to the agenda after the largely monochrome, anti-star culture of punk. Bowie was their hero and in 1983 they welcomed him back home.

The main problem, though, was that the new normalised Bowie was a very different beast from the sex-change style guru they remembered from only a few years before. He told *NME*'s Chris Bohn: "I don't have the urge to continue as a songwriter and performer in terms of experimentation – at this moment." The result was that 'Let's Dance', despite its classiness and accessibility, was a conservative record. The new mass audience it attracted would prove to be a huge hindrance to Bowie as the Eighties unfolded.

The album was re-released in 1995 with one bonus track.

MODERN LOVE

A sparkling opener, one of the best pop songs Bowie has written, and as different from Bowie's Enoesque late-Seventies introspection as you can get. A great spoken opening – 'I know when to go out/I know when to stay in/Get things done' – gets the ball rolling and there's that thunderous cyclical chorus (a re-write of the 1963 hit 'Tell Him', recorded by Billie Davis amongst others, and echoed by Bowie ten years later in 'Miracle Goodnight'), and some fine sax. One of the album's main lyrical themes, the relationship between God and man, comes through strongly too, with Bowie putting his trust in 'God and man' against formalised religion, which merely 'gets you to the church on time'. It was the third single to be taken off the album and reached a deserved Number 2 in the UK charts (Number 14 in the States).

CHINA GIRL

(BOWIE/POP)

More famous now for its video, depicting Bowie rolling around in the surf with a gorgeous Chinese girl; all bare buttocks and sandy bits, in a pastiche of Burt Lancaster in the film *From Here To Eternity*, this is in fact another fine pop song and his best Iggy Pop cover to date (the very different original can be found on Iggy's 1977 The Idiot album). Nile Rodgers serves up a cheeky little oriental riff for the beginning and Bowie croons admirably through this eminently hummable ditty. Its musical accessibility has, of course, helped to draw attention from the lyric's darker themes, dealing as they do with cultural imperialism and megalomania. Bowie screams 'I wander into town/Just like some sacred cow/visions of swastikas in my head/Plans for everyone/ It's in the white of my eyes'. A curious and incongruous lyric for the new 'normal' Bowie to resurrect, the single peaked at Number 2 in the UK and Number 10 in the States.

LET'S DANCE

Possibly Bowie's greatest ever-single (if not song) is this, the title track, in all its 7-minute 43-second glory. Musically it's simple, direct and emotional – and the big band-style arrangement, impassioned vocal delivery, thudding bass and killer hook made it an instant dance-floor staple. On the surface it appears lyrically naïve, but look closer and there's a hint of an impending apocalypse. The almost whispered delivery intones 'Let's Dance – for fear from grace should fall/Let's Dance – for fear tonight is all'. Is this the last dance before the bomb goes off? Had Bowie been listening to Prince's '1999' by any chance?

WITHOUT YOU

Essentially a filler, this is a very simple love song quite well sung.

RICOCHET

This is the only track on the album to contain the same gravitas as his Seventies work, although musically it is very different. Driven by a stark, military, indeed ricocheting drum figure it builds well with sax, horns and guitar. Lyrically again there's a religious theme as contemporary ills – 'the world is a corner waiting for jobs' – mean that we must 'turn the holy pictures so they face the wall'.

CRIMINAL WORLD

(GODWIN/BROWNE/LYONS)

This is a cover of a song from the little-known American post-punk outfit The Metros, which was fronted by Peter Godwin, and a fine version it is too with another excellent bass-line, some nice flute and one of the best couplets on the album: 'You caught me kneeling at your sister's door/That was no ordinary stick-up'!

CAT PEOPLE (PUTTING OUT FIRE)

(MORODER/BOWIE)

Bowie had written the lyrics to the theme for the 1982 film *Cat People* and the song had been a minor hit in April of that year, reaching Number 26 in the UK charts. This version replaces the Moroder sound with a dose of hard rock but fails to improve on what was already a pretty good original. Stevie Ray Vaughn's searing guitar lines dominate.

SHAKE IT

The album ends with the most dance-oriented track of the set. A cool, funky groove is the perfect backdrop to Bowie's fond-of-himself lyrics which directly echo the album's lunar and pugilistic leitmotif: 'I duck and I sway/I shoot at a full moon/So what's my line?'

BONUS TRACKS ON 1995 RE-ISSUE:

UNDER PRESSURE

Recorded with Queen in 1981, and a UK Number 1 to boot, this caused severe palpitations for many a Bowie fan, who could endure duets with Cher and Bing Crosby if only for kitsch value, but who regarded teaming up with Freddie and the lads as a fatal compromise with the mainstream. And, up to a point, they were right, as this collaboration led to some dire pairings as the Eighties went on. As a song it's not bad at all, and certainly not the disaster one might have feared. John Deacon's famously sampled bass-line holds it together, and Freddie and Bowie are both in fine fettle.

ZIGGY STARDUST: THE MOTION PICTURE

(ORIGINAL UK ISSUE: RCA PL 84862, RELEASED OCTOBER 1983; UK CD: EMI 0777 7 80411 2 2; US CD: RYKODISC RCD 40148; UK CHART: 17 [TOTAL WEEKS IN CHART: 6] US CHART: 89)

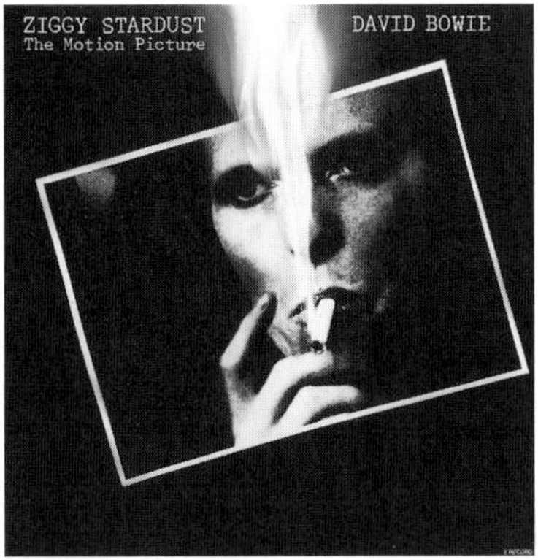

On July 3, 1973 the 'leper Messiah' finally bit the dust and so ended Bowie's first experiment in genetic pop engineering. At the time it was thought that Bowie had simply retired from the stage and his real reason for this temporary secession of live activities has become peculiarly entangled with his own myth. Bowie has gone on to say that he was merely retiring from playing Ziggy and that, since he had lived out his fictional character in real life, then it would only be fitting that he bury him in actuality too. In fact what happened

was that he needed a break, both from the non-stop schedule of touring, and from his band. Bowie had grown bored with the restraints the Spiders placed on him musically, and, with less rock-oriented projects probably already in mind, needed to free himself from the Jeff Beck-isms of Ronson and Co.

The resulting live album is probably only of interest to *aficionados*. That said, there's some fine moments, notably a medley of three of his best songs 'The Wild Eyed Boy From Freecloud/All The Young Dudes/Oh! You Pretty Thing', a rousing version of Jacques Brel's 'My Death' and the final Ziggy version of 'Rock'n'Roll Suicide' complete with last words: 'Bye bye we love you' and appropriate audience screams. Little did they know that this was only the beginning of Bowie's musical odyssey.

'White Light/White Heat', a cover of The Velvet Underground song, complete with Ronson's famously off-key guitar work, was released as a taster for the album and just missed the UK Top 40 at the end of 1983.

Full track listing: 'Hang On To Yourself', 'Ziggy Stardust', 'Watch That Man', 'Wild Eyed Boy From Freecloud'/'All The Young Dudes'/Oh! You Pretty Things', 'Moonage Daydream', 'Space Oddity', 'My Death' (Jacques Brel), 'Cracked Actor', 'Time', 'Width Of A Circle', 'Changes', 'Let's Spend The Night Together' (Mick Jagger/Keith Richards), 'Suffragette City', 'White Light/White Heat' (Lou Reed), 'Rock'n'Roll Suicide'.

TONIGHT

(ORIGINAL UK ISSUE: EMI AMERICA DB 1, RELEASED 24 SEPTEMBER 1984; RE-ISSUED 31 OCTOBER 1995 VIRGIN AMERICA; UK CD: EMI CDP 7 460472 2; UK CHART: 1 [TOTAL WEEKS IN CHART: 19]; US CHART: 11 [11])

If 'Let's Dance' and the subsequent Serious Moonlight tour had made Bowie bigger than ever in 1983, then 1984 saw the beginnings of a commercial and artistic free-fall that took the rest of the decade to halt. The global popular success of the new 'normal' Bowie, and the less-than radical musical soundtrack which accompanied this new model, proved to be his undoing. Bowie now had a sizeable mainstream following which he felt he needed to appease. In so doing, he lost sight of those very qualities (a sense of theatricality and adventure) which had won him support and respect in the first place, and began conscious-ly to distance himself from the cutting edge. His new audience, force-fed on a diet of Phil

Collins and Dire Straits, baulked at his theatricality on stage and his half-baked attempts at becoming mainstream on vinyl.

For 'Tonight', recorded at Le Studio, Morin Heights in Canada, Bowie was woefully short of new material and the album should never really have been released in this form, comprising as it did just two new songs of any note ('Loving The Alien' and 'Blue Jean'). Even Bowie himself, in a moment of almost painful self-realisation during an interview with Charles Shaar Murray to promote the album, recognised that he had lost the plot: "I feel on the whole fairly happy about my state of mind and my physical well-being and I guess I wanted to put my musical being in a similar staid and healthy area, but I'm not sure that that was a very wise thing to do."

'Tonight' just isn't up to the standard expected of Bowie: the production (courtesy of the three-man team of Bowie, Derek Bramble and Hugh Padgham) is lifeless, the performances below par, the music generally insipid and the arrangements wholly conventional. Even the promotional photographs for the album are truly awful, with the master of Seventies chic pictured wearing the kind of gaudy, tasteless suits and shirts that make your jaw drop in disbelief. Bowie's worst moment to date.

The 1995 re-issue came with three bonus tracks, making 'Tonight' much better value for money (the original was a paltry 36 minutes long), although, rather annoyingly, the demo of 'Loving The Alien', said by Bowie to be vastly superior to the finished version, is not included.

LOVING THE ALIEN

Although Bowie is rehashing an elderly theme (God as alien), this is the only track on the set to have any sense of grandeur or daring (or, 'Blue Jean' aside, a decent tune). Released as a single in May 1985 it peaked at number 19 in the UK with a much-criticised, though actually beautifully over-the-top video. Richard Skinner introduced it on *Top Of The Pops*, shaking his head in disgust at its supposed lavishness. Such was the anti-Bowie feeling at this point that even cloth-eared *TOTP* presenters felt moved to show their disapproval on screen!

DON'T LOOK DOWN

(POP/WILLIAMSON)

Despite Bowie's antipathetic stance towards the style in interviews, this cover version of an

Iggy Pop song is given a rather bland reggae treatment. Not at all bad though, as there is much worse to come...

GOD ONLY KNOWS

(BRIAN WILSON/TONY ASHER)

... like this. Apparently Bowie had recorded a very similar version back in 1973. Bowie is in full croon, and the rather ponderous orchestral arrangement is blandness personified.

TONIGHT

(BOWIE/POP)

The third cover version of the set has Bowie reconstructing Iggy Pop's tortured 1977 druggy epic into an extremely conventional, reggae-ish love song. Tina Turner is drafted in for a spot of duetting, but she remains totally buried in the mix. This was the album's second single, and surprisingly a complete flop, despite its pandering to the mainstream in such an obvious and rather galling way.

NEIGHBORHOOD THREAT

(BOWIE/POP)

Again Bowie decides to act as chief publicist for his mate Iggy with yet another cover version of an Osterberg oldie. The result is not at all bad, at least Bowie's vocal sounds half-awake, and the band rocks out in fine style.

BLUE JEAN

The only real contender for a hit single was this 'sexist piece of rock'n'roll' (Bowie's own words) and it made a respectable Number 6 in the UK. Musically it harks back to Ziggy-era Bowie and the accompanying video showed Bowie dripping in make-up for the first time since the great 'Ashes To Ashes'.

TUMBLE AND TWIRL

(BOWIE/POP)

On Iggy Pop's 'Blah Blah Blah' album of 1986, the Bowie/Pop co-creative juices were in full flow, with such classics as 'Shades' and 'Isolation', tracks which sounded more like Bowie than Bowie's own material did. With its vaguely Latin rhythms and half-baked lyrics, this is, however, a totally uninteresting foray into world music.

I KEEP FORGETTIN'

(LEIBER/ STOLLER)

This is a completely redundant cover version

of a poor song originally recorded by the American r'n'b artist Chuck Jackson. It is of absolutely no interest at all and sounds totally out of place even on this rambling album!

DANCING WITH THE BIG BOYS

(BOWIE/POP/ALOMAR)

Throughout the mid-Eighties Bowie was searching for a particular horn sound and this fractured piece of dance-pop is probably the closest he ever got to realising it. A far superior Arthur Baker re-mix can be found on the B-side of Jellybean's equally interesting twelve inch re-mix of 'Blue Jean' (EMI America 12 EA 181). That vinyl single is really all potential new Bowie fans need from this best-forgotten era.

BONUS TRACKS ON 1995 RE-ISSUE:

THIS IS NOT AMERICA

From the film *The Falcon And The Snowman* this is actually quite a successful team-up with snooze-jazz guitarist Pat Metheny. Lyrically it's not much cop but Bowie sings well and Metheny's soft-focus melody is affecting. The track hit Number 14 in the UK in early 1985 and was also one of Bowie's biggest-ever sellers in Germany.

ABSOLUTE BEGINNERS

Bowie's back to his finest form with this, the title song to the Julien Temple film of the same name. There's a wash of acoustic guitars, Rick Wakeman back tinkling his ivories and then Don Weller's fine saxophone solo, which almost shoves the air out of your chest when it blasts in towards the end. It just missed Number 1 in early 1986.

AS THE WORLD FALLS DOWN

Originally to be found on the 'Labyrinth' soundtrack this MOR ballad was slated for a pre-Christmas release in 1986, and might have been a big hit, but was shelved at the last minute.

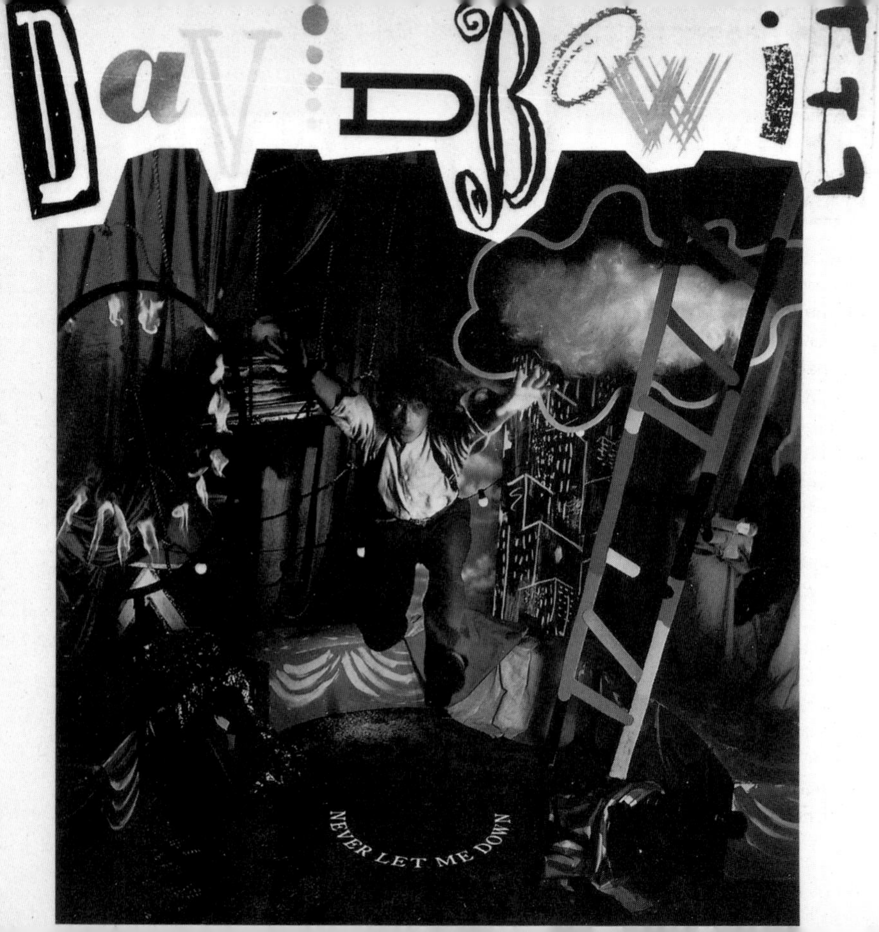
DAVID BOWIE
NEVER LET ME DOWN

NEVER LET ME DOWN

(ORIGINAL UK ISSUE: EMI AMERICA AMLS 3117, RELEASED 27 APRIL 1987; UK CD: EMI CDP 7 46677 2; RE-ISSUED 31 OCTOBER 1995 VIRGIN AMERICA, 13 NOVEMBER 1995, VIRGIN EUROPE; UK CHART: 6 [TOTAL WEEKS IN CHART: 16] US CHART: 34)

For the first time in his career Bowie was genuinely divorced from the cutting edge of popular music. An interview with Dave Thomas of *Today* in 1986 makes depressing reading: on music ("The music is so awful here... I've dropped out of radio, I play my old record collection"); on Live Aid ("I think the potential in Paul Young is extraordinary"); on his music ("Music starts to mellow... I don't have the riveting desire now to persuade people that what I have to say is right"); and finally on his audience ("What's the point of me trying to write for teenagers? The only way I could do that would be as some kind of father figure"). In short, Bowie had abdicated his position as Britain's most innovatory pop icon since The Beatles.

'Never Let Me Down', recorded at the Mountain Studios, Switzerland and co-produced by David Richards, is, not surprisingly, a fairly placid affair, but it does mark a step forward after the 'Tonight' debacle. Bowie was committed to a large-scale stadium tour the following year and attempted to write and record with that in mind. Long-standing side-kick Carlos Alomar and old school-chum and serious stadium rock axe-wielder Peter Frampton give the album an unspectacular AOR raucousness, but in the main the songs aren't up to the standard of old. Furthermore, Bowie sounds sonically distanced from the events; nowhere does the music actually sound like he has been involved with it, and in later interviews, he admits to being less than committed to the recording and arrangement of the album itself.

The Glass Spider tour of 1987, which showcased a large selection of current material, was almost universally panned, even though it offered a sense of adventure missing from the album. In fact the post-Live Aid period was absolutely the wrong climate for Bowie to work in. Guitar virtuosity and stadium rock were back, whilst indie-pop in Britain was going through a particularly barren back-to-basics phase. Only dance music in the form of house, rap and hip-hop showed the way forward, and Bowie's music sounded old and flat in comparison. Whatever, abseiling from the top of a sixty-foot fibre-glass neon-lit spider was definitely out, particularly if your new normalised audience had just been 'grooving' to Chris De Burgh in the car on the way to the gig.

DAY-IN DAY-OUT

This oddly jumbled, horn-driven rock/pop hybrid was the first single off the album, reaching Number 17 in the UK charts. Although by no means a classic Bowie single, the opening line, 'She was born in a handbag', is still a joy. The accompanying video, complete with a long-haired, roller-skating Bowie, caused a rumpus with its attempted rape and succession of sordid scenes from lowlife America, which purportedly mirrored the song's anti-Americanism. The video was re-edited for a number of television shows.

TIME WILL CRAWL

The strongest song on the album by a country mile was a surprisingly unsuccessful single peaking at a meek Number 33 in the UK. It harks back to Bowie's Seventies work in that the lyrics are able to fire the imagination without possessing any literal meaning in themselves. Good tune too. Bowie even performed the song on *Top Of The Pops*, ten years after his last visit to croon through 'Heroes', but the performance was never aired.

BEAT OF YOUR DRUM

There's a classic Bowie pop/rock song *à la* 'Jean Genie' somewhere in there, but it's buried in over-elaboration. There is a genuinely fine (and rather sexy) chorus, though: 'I'd like to beat on your drum/I'd like to blow on your horn'. Indeed, Mr Bowie! And there's yet another 'Speed Of Life' synth rip-off in the musical mix.

NEVER LET ME DOWN

(BOWIE/ALOMAR)

This song, a tribute to Bowie's personal aide Corrine 'Coco' Schwab, musically and lyrically pastiches John Lennon, particularly 'Jealous Guy'. It's actually a fine, if clichéd, pop song. The third single off the album, it hung around the UK Top 40 for a month but peaked at Number 34. It fared slightly better in the States, reaching Number 27.

ZEROES

The Beatles *leitmotif* is continued on this slick but rather lifeless pop song all about 'letting love in' and complete with mid-Sixties mantra at the end. The most interesting moment comes with the line 'And me, my little red corvette has driven by', in which Bowie name-checks a famous Prince song and simultaneously hands over the baton of experimentation to the Minneapolis midget. Touching in a way.

GLASS SPIDER

Although the howls of derision from critics are still echoing ten years on, this is one of the best tracks from Bowie's Eighties output. The song, telling a Freudian tale of a mother/child relationship in fantasy form, begins with a narration about a Glass Spider in the 'Zi Duang' province of an Eastern country and comes across, as most narrations do within pop, as incredibly pompous and embarrassing (who can fail to remember Phil Oakey on the Human League's 1986 American Number 1 'Human' or Telly Savalas's 'If'?), which should appal only those without a sense of humour. The song then stirs itself with a splendid riff and a great 'Gone, gone, the water's all gone' refrain.

SHINING STAR (MAKIN' MY LOVE)

This is a white, and rather polite, rap, featuring none other than actor Mickey Rourke, and would have been all the better if the awful, tinny-sounding arrangement had been beefed up a bit. Still, some signs of the old Bowie magic here – 'Life is like a broken arrow, memory a swinging door'.

NEW YORK'S IN LOVE

This is another nod to glories past (this time the ambient funk of Lodger's 'Red Sails'), but the production is flat and the song uninspired.

'87 AND CRY

This rocker, more than anything else on the album, indicated the direction his music would take with Tin Machine, although the lyrics, which desperately try and summon up some sort of anger and passion, are contrived and meaningless.

TOO DIZZY

(BOWIE/KIZILCAY)

This is the album's low point, a shameless AOR rocker which should have no place in the Bowie canon but, unfortunately, does.

BANG BANG

(POP/KRAAL)

'A couple of pence for a cup of tea for me old, starving, impecunious mate Iggy anyone?' Yet another in the long line of 'Bowie plays Pop' – but surely there were better tracks to cover than this.

BONUS TRACKS ON 1995 RE-ISSUE:

WHEN THE WIND BLOWS

The title track to Raymond Brigg's animated anti-nuke film feature a resurgent Bowie with an insistent, darkly foreboding guitar riff, great drumming, rousing orchestration and a polished vocal performance. It reached Number 44 in the UK late in November 1986 but deserved far better.

JULIE

This was originally the B-side to the 'Day In Day Out' single and would undoubtedly have made the better A-side. A catchy, simple song.

GIRLS

In contrast, this however just doesn't work at all. Bowie gets all hot and bothered in the vocal department but the song is a stiff.

TIN MACHINE

(ORIGINAL UK ISSUE: EMI-USA MTLS 1044, RELEASED 22 MAY 1989; UK CD: EMI CDP 7 91990 2; RE-ISSUED 31 OCTOBER 1995 VIRGIN AMERICA, 13 NOVEMBER 1995 VIRGIN EUROPE; UK CHART: 3 [TOTAL WEEKS IN CHART: 9] US CHART: 28)

By the late Eighties Bowie, or 'Dame David' as he was by then often dubbed, had become a figure of ridicule in the music press, and had been largely abandoned by his early-Eighties mainstream following. Bowie himself admitted that in the period 1983-86 he came close to calling it a day and returning to painting full-time. Obviously desperate measures were needed, and the Tin Machine project was a radical response to a dire situation.

In fact, Bowie's creative rebirth began not with the Tin Machine album but a year before at a charity gig for the Institute For Contemporary Arts at the Dominion Theatre, London. Here he performed a nine-minute version of the Lodger oldie 'Look Back In Anger' along with, amongst others, American guitarist Reeves Gabrels and Canadian Dance Troupe La La La Human Steps. The result was mesmeric, possibly Bowie's greatest performance since the Seventies in terms of sheer theatricality. Musically it was stripped down and at times veered towards heavy metal. It was this sound that Bowie developed with the Tin Machine project. On that day drum machine figures lent the music a contemporary edge, but for the new album Bowie opted for Hunt Sales on drums and Tony Sales on bass. Both had worked with Bowie on the Iggy Pop album Lust For Life. Gabrels was to be become Bowie's new right-hand man and the 'brains' (along with Bowie) to set against the 'balls' of the Sales brothers. Bowie also decided that Tin Machine was to be a fully-fledged band. Essentially a defensive measure, Bowie claimed to be simply one-quarter of a democratic whole, a move that was bound to founder sooner or later, much like Paul McCartney's intention of simply being a 'member' of Wings.

Produced by Tim Palmer and featuring Kevin Armstrong (who had worked with Bowie at Live Aid) on rhythm guitar, the album has gone down in rock history as a ghastly blunder. However, the reviews at the time were by no means uniformly poor, and the resulting album, fierce, spontaneous and uncompromising, is certainly a vast improvement on then recent solo outings. Forced to write quickly, often ad-libbing on mike, Bowie's lyrics have a tumbling stream-of-consciousness air, and the songs themselves often crash to a closure as if beheaded mid-verse. Bowie paraded a hectoring didacticism quite different to his other work, as tracks such as 'Crack City' and 'Under The God' deal with the evils of intoxicants and fascism respectively. It was hard not to read these songs as an exercise in catharism after his mid-Seventies flirtation with Nazi chic.

'Tin Machine', released at the height of interest in new metal groups such as Guns n'Roses, did reflect a musical Zeitgeist of sorts, and went on to sell a respectable million copies worldwide. However, by the late Eighties hard rock seemed an exhausted musical style, completely divorced from the cutting edge, and Tin Machine simply confirmed the redundancy of looking back to Cream, Hendrix and Led Zeppelin for inspiration. The sight of Bowie, now bearded, in a band with his mates, was the sort of laddish concept the androgynous outsider of the Seventies would have jeered at. Still, 'Tin Machine' will repay those potential Bowie fans willing to be taken on a brutal musical journey far away from the polished musical surfaces of Let's Dance.

HEAVEN'S IN HERE

An infectious bluesy riff, right out of the old school, drives this unashamed tale of hetero-sexual lust: 'Heaven lies between your marbled thighs'. Get the idea? Actually a good song and an incredible rootsy shock after the general tameness of 'Never Let Me Down'.

TIN MACHINE

(BOWIE/TONY SALES/HUNT SALES/REEVES GABRELS)

Another fine riff from Reeves Gabrels, and Bowie delivers his best vocal performance of the set in this song of self-disgust: 'Raging raging raging/ Burning in my room/Come on and get a good idea/Come on and get it soon'. Released as a double-A sided single with Dylan's 'Maggie's Farm', it reached Number 48 in the UK singles chart.

PRISONER OF LOVE

(BOWIE/TONY SALES/HUNT SALES/REEVES GABRELS)

Yes, another fine song, this time a rock ballad with hints of T.Rex's often-aped 'Children Of The Revolution' in the backing vocals. The first hint of didacticism creeps in with Bowie's exhortation to his addressee to 'Just stay square' in the face of life's excesses. The third single off the album, it failed to break the UK Top 75.

CRACK CITY

This is undoubtedly the most direct song Bowie has ever written on social issues, and its message is delivered with an unrestrained anger. Bowie graphically depicts the horrors of addiction, rounding on the drug-pusher at the song's dénouement – 'May the ho-ho hounds of paranoia/Dance upon your stinking bed'. Musically, the song borrows from 'Wild Thing', originally by The Troggs, although famously covered by Hendrix. The purpose of this particular musical borrowing is to simplistically bring into the listener's mind one of the most resonant paradigms of rock-and-roll death through intoxicant abuse (regardless of the actual circumstances of the great man's death).

I CAN'T READ

(BOWIE/REEVES GABRELS)

Possibly the best song on the album, this arty, discordant number is a distillation of one of Bowie's obsessions: an inability to feel. After the monosyllabic delivery of most of the song, Bowie screams: 'I can't read shit any more'. His vocal delivery renders the line highly ambiguous, in that it actually sounds like 'I can't reach it any more', thus becoming a comment on his recent musical paralysis.

UNDER THE GOD

Musically, this slab of hard rock re-works The Mojo's 'I Wish You Would' (a song Bowie had covered on 'Pin-Ups'). It is a further view of the new, politicised Bowie, dealing as it does with the rise of neo-Nazism. A poor choice as a lead-off single, it reached a paltry Number 51 in the UK.

AMAZING

(BOWIE/REEVES GABRELS)

This, the simplest song on the album, is also one of the best. A love song no less, with one of those ascending melodic lines that has become a Bowie trademark. The obvious choice as a single, it remains an album cut only.

WORKING CLASS HERO

(JOHN LENNON)

Tin Machine owed a debt to Lennon's earlier politicking, and this is obviously intended as a homage to that cause. However, this cover replaces the acoustic spite of the original with an overbearing posturing.

BUS STOP

(BOWIE/REEVES GABRELS)

This short and rather silly song about a man who finds God at the bus stop, displays a Bowie in fine full-cockney regalia.

PRETTY THING

This is the weakest song in the set, the band power on remorselessly and Bowie sings as if in search of a decent tune. And the 'Tie me down, pretend you're Madonna' line is crass.

VIDEO CRIMES

(BOWIE/TONY SALES/HUNT SALES)

As on 'I Can't Read', Bowie ransacks his late-Seventies period for more blanked-out numbness. Interesting, but it doesn't quite work.

RUN

(KEVIN ARMSTRONG/BOWIE)

This track has very little of Bowie's personality stamped on it but it's pleasant enough with some pretty guitar work.

SACRIFICE YOURSELF

(BOWIE/TONY SALES/HUNT SALES)

Another dose of heavy metal bluster but by now it's all wearing very thin: more guitars, more advice for the potentially misguided. The musical is monotone and the message old.

BABY CAN DANCE

This song could have been a fine Bowie rocker had it not been subjected to a rather tawdry guitar freak-out from Gabrels at the end. Here is the best chorus on the album, and the Stones-inspired rhythm-and-blues shuffling beat ought to have secured a better result.

BONUS TRACK ON 1995 RE-ISSUE:

COUNTRY BUS STOP

Mildly aggravating country and western version of one of the album's better cuts.

TIN MACHINE II

(UK CD: LONDON 8282721; RELEASED 2 SEPTEMBER 1991; UK CHART: NO.23 [TOTAL WEEKS IN CHART: 3])

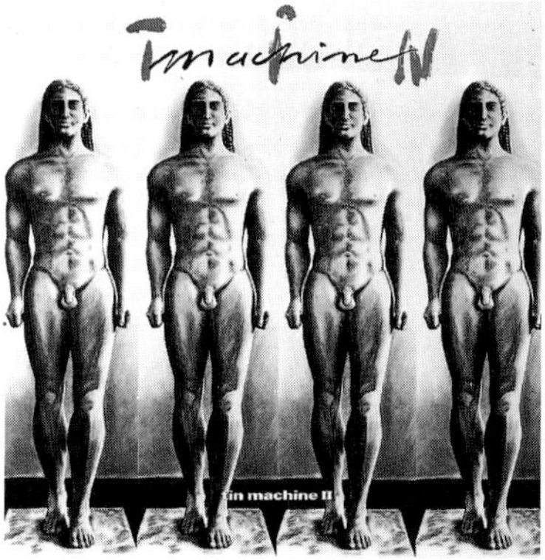

Although, with the first 'Tin Machine' album, Bowie had partially succeeded in transfusing some purpose into his music after his mid-Eighties coma, the follow-up was a decidedly mixed bag. The radical metal approach was diluted and the result was a half-baked Bowie solo album compromised by the muso-meanderings of his partners in crime.

Mainly recorded in Australia in late 1989 (three tracks were cut in England in March 1991), its release was delayed for two pressing reasons. First of all, Bowie agreed to the buy-me-again Sound + Vision tour, in which he tackled his big hits for what he promised would be the last time. He assembled a tight Tin Machine-style 'back to basics' group who failed to give his back catalogue the intricate finesse it demanded. Visually, however, the shows were stunning, being the first to use interactive video techniques in stadia. These shows served as a stark contrast to the chain-smoking, bearded rocker, power-chording his way through the previous year's Tin Machine tour. Secondly, sometime during 1990, Bowie and EMI fell out. Rumour has it that, presented with the tapes to 'Tin Machine II', EMI decided to pull the plug. Apart from 'Let's Dance', Bowie's EMI material had veered from the good to the atrocious (by Bowie's standards) and it now seemed likely that the Company had simply had enough.

So when 'Tin Machine II' came out in the autumn of 1991 on the London label, Bowie's recording career seemed not simply to have stalled, but to have gone into reverse. It garnered what are politely called 'mixed reviews' (NME actually liked it!) before slipping out of the charts after a paltry three weeks, despite extensive media promotion (including two *Top Of The Pops* appearances, a Radio 1 session and a short world tour). Most Bowie fans simply hated seeing their idol in a lime-green suit in a rock band with the lads. 'Tin Machine II' sounded compromised and diluted, with Hunt and Tony Sales pulling the more sentient Bowie and Gabrels into more traditional American rock areas. It was obvious from that moment on that Bowie was unhappy with Tin Machine's 'democracy' and would be forced to resume his solo career again.

Largely a set for die-hard Bowie fans only, and rock fans at that, the album did have a few worthwhile moments in amongst the stodge, not least the stomping opener...

BABY UNIVERSAL

(LYRICS BOWIE: MUSIC BOWIE/GABRELS)

This frantic three-minute rocker was the second single off the album, scraping to Number 49 in the UK charts. Reminiscent of something from 'Scary Monsters', though without that album's studied weirdness, it's a fine, under-valued song.

ONE SHOT

(LYRICS BOWIE: MUSIC BOWIE/GABRELS/ H. SALES/T. SALES)

This slab of AOR hard rock is catchy enough, but an awfully indulgent guitar solo and some unnervingly sexist lyrics – 'One thing led to a dead end/One shot put her away hey-hey' – sink it. It was a single in Europe and Australia only.

YOU BELONG IN ROCK'N'ROLL

(LYRICS BOWIE: MUSIC BOWIE/GABRELS)

Two decades earlier, in 'Changes', Bowie the poseur had urged , 'Look out all you rock-'n'rollers'. Now, sadly, Bowie himself was beginning to resemble that which he had set out to replace. This is far from being a poor song though, containing as it does some understated guitar work for once, with Bowie doing a hammy Elvis impersonation. Mistakenly released as a single, it limped to Number 33 (Tin Machine's highest chart placing in the UK singles charts).

IF THERE IS SOMETHING

(FERRY)

Originally to be found on Roxy Music's epoch-making first album, here the song is totally de-ironised and rather blandly presented in accordance with Tin Machine's general crash-bang-wallop approach.

AMLAPURA

(LYRICS BOWIE: MUSIC BOWIE/GABRELS)

This stately, acoustic piece works well, although hardly breaks new ground. 'Amlapura', a district in Bowie's beloved Bali in Indonesia, was the site of a massive volcanic eruption in 1963 – hence, presumably, 'all the dead children buried standing'. Incidentally, an alternative version, with Bowie singing in Indonesian, can be found on the 'You Belong In Rock and Roll' CD single.

BETTY WRONG

(LYRICS BOWIE: MUSIC BOWIE/GABRELS)

This is pretty dull. Bowie and Gabrels try to be understated and wistful, but the song isn't up to it.

YOU CAN'T TALK

(LYRICS BOWIE, MUSIC BOWIE/GABRELS/ H. SALES/T. SALES)

Musically this track re-treads 'Never Let Me Down''s 'New York's In Love' (not the richest musical vein for cannibalisation, one would have thought) and the whole thing is easily forgettable.

STATESIDE

(LYRICS H.SALES/BOWIE: MUSIC H.SALES/BOWIE)

This geriatric blues number must be the nadir of Bowie's recording career to date. Hunt Sales takes the lead vocal and bawls out 'I'm going Stateside with my convictions', while Bowie's attempt to rescue the situation in the chorus with some rather unconvincing irony makes it all worse. The most alarming thing is that this crass homage to American authenticity makes a mockery of everything Bowie had stood for. Dreadful.

SHOPPING FOR GIRLS

(LYRICS BOWIE: MUSIC BOWIE/GABRELS)

Just when the whole set appears to have ground to a halt, Bowie goes some way toward rescuing it with this quite excellent piece of reportage. Whereas on the first Tin Machine album his 'protest' songs came across as sermonising, now, without playing the heavy-handed father figure, Bowie blankly recites a liturgy of atrocities (based on a news report from Reeves Gabrels' journalist wife) against a neat guitar riff.

A BIG HURT

This was probably the only occasion where Tin Machine got the dumb hard rock pose right (and significantly it's on a track Bowie composed alone). There's a fabulous chorus and although it's still just a piece of sexist rock-and- roll, Bowie's almost comedic vocal performance carries the whole thing off.

SORRY

(LYRICS AND MUSIC: H. SALES)

Sloshy, repetitive, sub-Bryan Adams ballad sung by Hunt Sales. Another bummer from the drummer, and yes, you weren't the only one who was sorry, Hunt.

GOODBYE MR ED

(LYRICS BOWIE: MUSIC BOWIE/H.SALES/T.SALES)

How can someone responsible for such execrable schmaltz as 'Sorry' then have a hand in writing what is probably the finest Bowie track never to be released as a single? This is quite simply a great pop song. Bowie's resigned vocals relay a series of observations about the built-in nostalgia of contemporary American culture over a beautiful melody, reminiscent of, of all things, Acker Bilk's 1961 mega instrumental hit 'Stranger On The Shore'. This fine song, concluding an album that few pop fans will ever get round to listening to, is destined to remain an undiscovered gem.

'Tin Machine II' actually ends with an uncredited minute-long instrumental with Bowie's saxophone to the fore. It's an edit of a track called 'Hammerhead', to be found on the 'You Belong In Rock And Roll' CD single (London CD 305), but it's not essential Bowie material.

TIN MACHINE LIVE: OY VEY, BABY

(ORIGINAL UK ISSUE: VICTORY MUSIC 828 328 1, RELEASED 27 JULY 1992; UK CD: VICTORY 828 328 2.)

Never was a Bowie-related project awaited with so little interest as this, Tin Machine's third, live, album. Mixed by Reeves Gabrels it accurately captures what Tin Machine were all about live – noisy guitars, thumping drums, socio-political songs and little else. Whilst it was refreshing to see Bowie close-up in small auditoria after a decade of stadium gigging, the band made Bowie sound hoarse and ordinary as a singer. Listening to Gabrels' live mix Bowie is reported to have commented that the album sounded like 'deconstructionist R & B'. However, to most people it sounded old hat and dispensable. The track listing is totally predictable (Tin Machine had quite successfully covered The Pixies' 'Debaser' on tour, which would have made an interesting curio if included) and, 'Goodbye Mr Ed' and an extended re-work of 'You Belong In Rock And Roll' aside, this is, sadly, completely superfluous. And we are not even spared the dreaded 'Stateside'. Incidentally, the title is a 'side-splitting' pun on U2's towering Achtung Baby. If only it had a tenth of that record's wit and invention.

Full track listing: 'If There Is Something' (Ferry), 'Amazing', 'I Can't Read', 'Stateside', 'Under The God', 'Goodbye Mr Ed', 'Heaven's In Here', 'You Belong In Rock & Roll'.

DAVID BOWIE
BLACK TIE WHITE NOISE

BLACK TIE WHITE NOISE

(UK CD: ARISTA 74321136972, US CD: SAVAGE 74785/50212/2; RELEASED APRIL 5 1993; REISSUED 31 OCTOBER 1995 VIRGIN AMERICA; UK CHART: 1 [TOTAL WEEKS IN CHART: 11])

According to the 'official line' given by Bowie in interviews to promote 'Black Tie White Noise' during the first half of 1993, the impetus for his first solo record in six years was his 1992 marriage to Iman, the Somalian-born model (she of the Tia Maria ad in the Eighties), and this exercise had opened up a flood of ideas and emotions that go to make this album his best since 'Scary Monsters'. In reality, however, although the desire to write his own wedding music (a preserve of the very wealthy and very talented if ever there was) might have kick-started the creative process, a solo album had been planned for several years. Tracks had been laid down around late 1990 with members of Bryan Adams' band, but never released. Quite what that bizarre mis-match actually produced has mercifully never seen the light of day, except for a cover of Dylan's 'Like A Rolling Stone', to be found on Mick Ronson's solo album 'Heaven And Hull' (Sony, 474742 2) released in 1994.

Also, outside the Tin Machine project, Bowie had guested on Adrian Belew's 1990 album 'Young Lions' (Atlantic, 7 82099 2), penning the infectious and unjustly overlooked 'Pretty Pink Rose' and co-writing the inessential 'Gunman'. The commercial failure of Tin Machine, and, perhaps more importantly, the restriction the band must have placed on Bowie in terms of control of the final product, led directly to him once again stepping into the limelight as a solo artist. In 1995 Bowie told *Interview* magazine that he saw the Tin Machine phase as a necessary, if painful, period of self-evaluation: "Once I had done Tin Machine, nobody could see me any more. They didn't know who the hell I was, which was the best thing that ever happened, because I was back using all the artistic pieces that I needed to survive and I was imbuing myself with the passion that I had in the late Seventies."

The slate wiped clean, he resumed his solo career with an overtly commercial offering. Bowie has mythologised his career in order to give the impression that he has always been a cult artist, has never sold many records, and has never wanted mainstream popularity, but at various stages he has always back-pedalled and gone for the mainstream by the jugular.

Nile Rodgers was once again brought in as producer, but 'Black Tie White Noise' is no re-run of 'Let's Dance'. Whereas on that album Bowie sounded as if he was guesting on a Nile Rodgers/Chic-inspired Bowie album, on the sequel it is Bowie who is calling the shots, with Rodgers helping to put the action onto tape with a commercial sheen.

And there is action a-plenty. For a start Bowie sings wonderfully well, giving perhaps his best vocal performance yet. On the more recent tours his vocals had shown signs of strain and he had lost some of his upper range – hardly surprising after years of almost constant gigging and nicotine abuse. On 'Black Tie White Noise' the songs fit the voice perfectly, however, and Bowie's lower, richer, rounded vocal is just the ticket. The musical fabric is dense and alive, with Lester Bowie's excellent trumpet playing taking over the role of soloist from lead guitar, and Bowie's asthmatic sax-playing also to the forefront. This is also the first Bowie album for a decade actually to sound up with the game, bass-heavy dance structures well to the fore in most songs. It is also, 'Young Americans' aside, Bowie's 'blackest' album to date. In fact it was conceived as a musical re-creation of, and comment on, not only the racial mix in his own marriage but also the active creative process which had long infused his work: taking 'black' styles and overlaying a European melodic sensibility.

Whilst the album still falls a little way short of his best Seventies work (the sense of desperation infused with megalomania which made his earlier work often spine-chilling is simply not there), three tracks at the heart of the set – 'Jump They Say', 'Nite Flights' and 'Pallas Athena' – provide a musical trio worthy of comparison with any moment from his Seventies work.

Early 1993 should have been an extremely propitious time for a new Bowie album. Seattle-grunge denim-clad anonymity was giving way in the UK to arty, camp, laddish 'Britpop' and some excellent new groups such as Blur, Suede, The Auteurs and Pulp, all of whom carried echoes of Bowie somewhere in their music, their packaging, or their approach to music-making. Suede in particular, fronted by Brett 'a bisexual man who has never had a homosexual experience' Anderson, borrowed heavily from the Ziggy-era's glam-slam, and it must have given Bowie some satisfaction to see 'Black Tie White Noise' depose their début Suede album from the top of the UK charts on its first week of release. However, from that moment on, it was all downhill for the Bowie comeback. In America he had signed with the small Savage label, which promptly went bust at the time of the album's release, seriously affecting promotion and distribution. Bowie's decision not to tour the album must have significantly affected sales too. Also the Bowie camp, now renowned for not being able to pick a single for toffee, blundered badly by relegating the outrageously catchy 'Miracle Goodnight' to third-choice single release. Had that led off the campaign, the album would surely have become one of Bowie's biggest sellers.

THE WEDDING

The opener, an instrumental up-date of one of the pieces composed for that wedding, is one of three quite excellent instrumentals to be found on the album. Since Bowie's family were Church of England and Iman's Muslim, Bowie wanted to create a piece of music which mixed the two elements. Church bells open the track, giving way to an infectious bass-line, with some great melismatic sax work by Bowie giving that 'eastern' touch.

YOU'VE BEEN AROUND

(BOWIE/GABRELS)

This song had been played live, in a radically different form, by Tin Machine, but never released. It's another strong song – the 'real' Bowie vocal only cuts in after the first verse's treated vocal. Bowie's self-mocking, self-referential 'Ch-ch-ch-ch-changed' line, some great trumpet by Lester Bowie, and a glorious bassline add up to a delight. Reeves Gabrels does solo at the end of the track but, rather naughtily, is mixed so far down by Bowie (in what might have been a deliberate gesture of defiance against the democracy of Tin Machine) that he is barely audible above the rhythm track!

I FEEL FREE

(BRUCE/BROWN)

A cover version to send purists running for that CD remote control fast forward button but which actually works rather well. Bowie completely reconstructs the song into a rocky techno freak-out and Mick Ronson makes his last performance on a Bowie album with a fine guitar solo.

Bowie's vocal is hilariously deep at one stage too, causing severe aural distress, one might imagine, to dogs, cats, budgies and the like.

BLACK TIE WHITE NOISE

Inspired by the LA riots this is Bowie back on 'I told you so' mode, and duetting with soul singer Al B Sure! It's a good enough song but, call me an old cynic, my idea of what Bowie is about just doesn't fit with the moralising man presented on this track, even if we all agree with the general sentiments of striving for racial harmony and strength through recognising (and respecting) cultural difference.

JUMP THEY SAY

This is simply a fine pop song, undoubtedly a classic Bowie single, and a welcome UK Top 10 hit after a seven-year gap. Thematically it draws on the life (and death) of Bowie's step-brother Terry, who committed suicide in 1985. Musically the song has the same repetitive drive which characterises so much of his best work, a backwards sax line again adds an 'Eastern' wailing quality, and Bowie's cautionary/predictive vocals ('They say jump', 'Watch out!') give the song a chilling cinematic quality. The video is superb too.

NITE FLIGHTS

(ENGELS)

The disquiet of 'Jump They Say' is continued in this excellent cover of The Walker Brothers' 'Nite Flights' (originally from the 1978 album of the same name). It's a hard-edged dance track with Bowie's brooding vocals and a soaring speaker-to-speaker synth line amongst its many charms.

PALLAS ATHENA

The second instrumental on the album is probably the best of a very good three. A sombre violin line gives way to the sort of experimental dance music Bowie should do more of, with both Bowies soloing to good effect. For all you budding Bowiephiles, Pallas Athene (or Minerva) was, according to Brewer's book of Myth and Legend, fabled to have sprung, with a tremendous battle-cry, fully armed from the brain of Jupiter. Ouch!

MIRACLE GOODNIGHT

The catchiest track on the album, based around an ever-circling riff which, as Bowie commented, 'just keeps coming and coming'. There's a great synthesised orchestral break in the middle and even some hi-life guitar. I have it on good authority from someone who lived in Bali that the five-note riff which runs through the track sounds exactly like the Balinese frog chorus at night. Having heard a tape of the aforementioned frogs, I have to agree!

DON'T LET ME DOWN AND DOWN

(TARHA/VALMONT)

The tone of the album, which was lightened by 'Miracle Goodnight', continues in much the same vein for the rest of the set. It's a good slowie, nothing outstanding, apart from Bowie's strangely accented vocals.

LOOKING FOR LESTER

In which Nile and Dame David bring jazz to the pop masses. Although not a jazz fan myself, I became more interested in the genre (which goes to show how impressionable I am) after listening to this groovy track, which sets three solos (from Lester Bowie, Bowie and the re-called Mike Garson) against a slab of thudding techno. An incongruous success.

I KNOW IT'S GONNA HAPPEN SOMEDAY

(MORRISSEY/NEVIN)

The original Morrissey track (to be found on the Mick Ronson-produced 'Your Arsenal' album of 1992) ended with a re-run of the dénouement of Bowie's own classic 'Rock'n'Roll Suicide'. Bowie's version is thus a homage to a homage (making it a postmodernist's dream text) but, rather inexplicably, leaves out the slice of 'Rock'n'Roll Suicide' Mozza had originally sampled. It's a not altogether successful cover. Bowie is a little too studiously melodramatic in his attempt to produce a 'Young Americans'-era vocal and piano mix, and the whole serves to remind all Bowie fans of just what a great lyricist Morrissey has become (better, it has to be said, than Bowie himself at the time). Would have made an acceptable single, though.

THE WEDDING SONG

Here Bowie admits to having deliberately written a clichéd, gushing, saccharine-sweet love song for his bride. This is basically the opening track with words on, and it's fine in itself, though inferior to the instrumental version. Still, an effective way to end the 'official' set.

JUMP THEY SAY

(ALTERNATE MIX)

Superfluous, inferior version with some orgasmic moans from one of the backing singers added into the mix.

LUCY CAN'T DANCE

Although a little over-long to be singles material, this is another highly catchy piece of undemanding pop. It would have overshadowed almost everything on Bowie's previous two solo offerings and this fact alone gives some indication of how far he had gone in raising the standard of his work with this album.

THE BUDDHA OF SUBURBIA

(UK CD: ARISTA 74321 170042, RELEASED 8 NOVEMBER 1993; ISSUED 31 OCTOBER 1995; US: VIRGIN AMERICA; UK CHART: 87)

When the BBC planned to turn Hanif Kureishi's excellent 1990 novel and Whitbread Prize winner *The Buddha Of Suburbia* into a television play, it was particularly fitting that Bowie was asked to provide the music. The novel deals with issues of race, sexuality and stardom in the Seventies, and Bowie as a cultural icon was drawn upon for the construction of one of the characters, Charlie, who rifles through a succession of personae – from hippy to glam rocker to punk before relocating, Billy Idol-style, to the States.

The most important point to make is that this is not a soundtrack album, despite the legend on the album's front cover. The music here completely reconstructs the incidental music used in the BBC adaptation – this is a bona fide solo offering. Its extremely poor chart showing is probably attributable to three factors: firstly the album was released at the same time as EMI put out 'Bowie: The Singles Collection' and thus got lost in the pre-Christmas retro-rush. Secondly, the mis-marketing of the album as a soundtrack obviously confused potential buyers already warned off by similar artistic failures in that area before, not least Bowie's own half-baked 'Labyrinth' project. And lastly, Bowie did very little in the way of interviews to promote the damn thing. 'The Buddha Of Suburbia' therefore stands as the great lost Bowie album. Recorded in a mere six days, and co-produced with David Richards, on it Bowie shares instrumental duties with multi-instrumentalist Erdal Kizilcay, who had played on the previous two Bowie tours. Veteran Bowie-man Mike Garson provides piano for 'South Horizon' and 'Bleed Like A Craze, Dad'.

What gives the album its real clout is Bowie's apparent sense of liberation after 'Black Tie White Noise' had at least partially replenished his commercial stock. He had always been wont to recycle his own musical past and now this stealing was legitimised and became the *raison d'être* of the project. So it's no surprise that some of the tracks sound uncannily like either lost Ziggy recordings (e.g. the title track) or homages to his Seventies contemporaries (e.g. the late-Seventies Roxy Music-sounding 'Strangers When We Meet'). Again, like 'Black Tie White Noise', this is not Bowie at the peak of his creative powers, but it stands head and shoulders above both Tin Machine's albums and his post-'Let's Dance' solo material.

The CD booklet contains an essay by Bowie on the project, his influences and working procedures, and an assessment of the state of pop in the Nineties. A bizarre read, it looks like an attempt by Bowie to match Eno's pop culture analysis. It ends with a piece of flag-waving which re-establishes Bowie's Englishness in the wake of 'Britpop'. Here is a taste of the invective: "We have so much un-nurtured talent in this country it borders on the criminal", whilst "In America popular music has never been more divisive, both racially and socially". Whether all this will lead to a rival to Paul McCartney's 'Fame'-style Institute For Performing Arts and to Bowie actually investing in developing talent on a large scale is another matter entirely. The Institute For Posing and Pretentiousness would be a great idea though.

The album was given its first release outside of the UK in October 1995 and came with new art work.

BUDDHA OF SUBURBIA

Peaking at a miserly Number 35 in the UK chart, this is a fine, stirring 'Bewlay Brothers' meets

'Absolute Beginners' title track. Bowie sings in his best 'cokernee', the music quotes 'Space Oddity' and the lyrics 'All The Madmen'. An almost perfect pastiche.

SEX AND THE CHURCH

You'd be hard pushed to call this one a song in any conventional sense. Based on a slow funky groove, there's also a debonair jazzy touch, and Bowie's vocals are suitably incantatory.

SOUTH HORIZON

Bowie's favourite track on the album showcases some beautiful piano work from Garson on a fractured jazz instrumental which splits in two halfway through.

THE MYSTERIES

This instrumental is the closest Bowie has come to a solo ambient instrumental *à la* Eno. It has what sounds like a backwards slowed-down piano providing the main musical information.

BLEED LIKE A CRAZE, DAD

This track has a marked cinematic feel and Bowie's oddly delivered white rap style makes for an incongruous, though successful, mix.

STRANGERS WHEN WE MEET

This really does sound like 'Flesh And Blood'-era Roxy Music and, whilst boasting a catchy melody, was probably a little too pedestrian to be chosen as a single at this stage. It was re-recorded for the 'Outside' album and finally issued as a double A-sided single in November 1995 (with a live version of 'The Man Who Sold The World').

DEAD AGAINST IT

Another powerful track, this time with a late-Seventies new-wave feel and a wonderful cyclical synthesised coda.

UNTITLED NO.1

Probably the strongest cut on the album, this is a glorious piece of early Seventies retro-mysticism, with a haunting melody and some rather silly Marc Bolan bleats at the end. Stunning, and should have been a single.

IAN FISH, U.K. HEIR

This instrumental is certain to send 'Let's Dance'-era Bowie fans fleeing in panic. Bowie, playing around with form and content in traditional ambient style, loads a funereally slow re-tread of the musical motifs of the title track with copious dollops of surface static. Almost unlistenable, but intriguingly so.

BUDDHA OF SUBURBIA

Lastly, a completely superfluous, and almost identical, re-run of the first track, with the much-loathed Lenny Kravitz on guitar (but why?).

SANTA MONICA '72

(UK CD: TRIDENT INTERNATIONAL : GOLDEN YEARS GY 002; US CD LIMITED EDITION: GRIFFIN MUSIC 357; RELEASED 25 APRIL 1994; UK CHART: 74)

Before its official release, this was probably the most sought-after Bowie bootleg, and it's not difficult to see why. Originally a live FM radio broadcast from the Civic Auditorium, Santa Monica, on October 20 1972, this is a must for serious Bowie collectors. Bowie and the Spiders give a fine performance and this album trashes 'Ziggy Stardust: The Motion Picture' in terms of overall musicality if not historical significance. The CD can be found in a number of different editions.

Full track listing: 'Intro', 'Hang On To Yourself', 'Ziggy Stardust', 'Changes', 'The Supermen', 'Life On Mars?', 'Five Years', 'Space Oddity', 'Andy Warhol', 'My Death',

'The Width Of A Circle', 'Queen Bitch', 'Moonage Daydream', 'John I'm Only Dancing', 'Waiting For The Man', 'The Jean Genie', 'Suffragette City', 'Rock'n'Roll Suicide'.

DAVID BOWIE
1.OUTSIDE

OUTSIDE

(UK CD: RCA 74321 31066 2, RELEASED SEPTEMBER 25 1995 US CD: VIRGIN AMERICA 7243 840712/7; UK CHART: 8; US CHART: 21)

For years it seemed a good bet that Bowie and Eno would never work together again. During the late Eighties, while Eno was making his fortune as U2's producer and being rehabilitated as the ambient godfather and Bowie was dabbling in hard rock, it looked as if musically the two ex-collaborators were light years apart. Bowie was going for a live, band sound, while Eno had never been interested in using the recording process as a means of capturing 'real' performances.

The first hint of a team-up came in October 1992 when this writer managed to quiz Eno in Munich during one of his (always very good) lectures. If memory serves me right, he told me that Bowie had been asked to write a piece of music to commemorate the twelve hundredth anniversary of the institution of the city of Kyoto, and that Bowie had asked him, Eno, to collaborate. Nought came of this, but it was obvious that Eno was finding Bowie's increasingly textural music more to his liking. Around the beginning of 1994 they started work on what would eventually become 'Outside'.

'Outside' is littered with references to Bowie's musical past, particularly the under-rated 'Lodger' and the still towering 'Diamond Dogs'. The really astonishing thing about it is the way in which Bowie has been able to re-summon all the paranoia, pomposity, and eclecticism of his Seventies work so utterly convincingly,once again proving adept at ransacking images from high art and playfully bastardising them through his music. On 'Outside' the preoccupation is with ritual art and neo-paganism. In the Nineties Bowie's own dabbling in art became less a hobby and more a vocation. He became a member of the editorial board of the magazine *Modern Painters*, began befriending figures such as the British artist Damien Hirst (famed for exhibiting a dead sheep in a tank of formaldehyde), and in 1995 exhibited his own paintings and sculptures for the first time. The video for the first single 'Hearts Filthy Lesson' says it all. Directed by Samuel Bayer, who made Nirvana's famous video for 'Smells Like Teen Spirit', it shows a Bowie surrounded by almost holocaust-like images of deprivation: hangings, decapitations, his own body of flesh and blood covered in powder paint as if bodily fluids, skin and paint have somehow been mixed to form one primeval medium.

'Outside' is probably Bowie's bleakest album yet (and that's saying a lot). It deals with the murder of Baby Grace Blue, a 14-year-old victim of an 'art crime' (her innards having been exhibited as art) and the investigation into the death by Professor Nathan Adler, art detective. After years of avoiding overt characterisation on stage and on record, Bowie went wild on 'Outside', creating and impersonating other figures too, such as the 22-year-old prime suspect Leon Blank, a 78-year-old art-drug and DNA print dealer Algeria Touchshriek, the omnipotent leading lady Ramona A Stone, and the Minotaur! In typical Bowie fashion this is a concept album with the concept left out. There is a narrative of sorts, but its direction and the extent to which the William Burroughs-styled cut-ups are actually meant to convey any literal meaning, is open to debate. And in truth, it's hard to get that involved in the story in the first place. Whereas Ziggy's cartoon-like imagery instantly struck a chord and 'Diamond Dogs' proffered a re-write of a familiar novel, 'Outside''s obsessions are likely to remain mainly those of their creator.

All this chicanery left Bowie, as always, open to accusations of wild pretentiousness from the 'authenticity' wing of the British media, those writers who, for some perverse reason, think pop should be simple and orthodox, anti-commercialistic, anti-showbusiness and, above all, true to its roots in black music, and should not be allowed to rise above its station and become an art form. However, accusing Bowie of pretentiousness is like accusing Maradona of kicking a football. Moreover, for the first time since 'Scary Monsters', much of the music was so inventive that Bowie's detractors looked like musical Luddites and ultimately rather silly.

In the end, 'Outside' was, on balance, well-received by the press. Long-time Bowie-watcher Charles Shaar Murray called it 'a mad, bad, dangerous album, by turns, chilling, pretty, ugly, scary, gripping and vastly intriguing' and even the British inkies, *Melody Maker* and *NME*, who had been on Bowie's back for over a decade, gave grudgingly good notices too.

'Outside', mooted to be the first of a five-CD

cycle taking us into the new millennium, is a mud-pie of styles from jungle and techno to avant-garde jazz. There are a couple of lame moments (and the narrative sections sometimes hit a seven out of ten on the Bowie Cringeometer), but whereas, for example, 'The Buddha Of Suburbia' had four genuinely great tracks, 'Outside' has more than twice as many. There's some fine drumming from Soul Asylum's Sterling Campbell, some funky and instantly recognisable rhythm guitar from Carlos Alomar, and Reeves Gabrels, ex-Tin Machine, puts in some excellent work too. The lead instrumentalist, however, is Mike Garson, although his piano contributions are at times overdone and lose their cranky emotive power. And of course, there's Eno everywhere in the mix with some of the most wonky, nutty and dangerous sounds you'll ever hear on CD. 'Outside', which comes complete with a booklet containing an excerpt from the 'Nathan Adler Diaries' (a largely and deliberately impenetrable Bowie narrative) and a succession of computer images which show Bowie morphed into the album's characters, is another essential Bowie purchase.

All lyrics are by Bowie, while he shares most of the musical credits with Eno and Gabrels (Garson, Kizilcay, and Campbell are also credited on some tracks, and Kevin Armstrong, Bowie's guitarist at Live Aid and on the Tin Machine tour of 1989 is credited on the title track).

LEON TAKES US OUTSIDE

'Outside' begins with this almost incantatory jumble of sound and monologue as the scene is set temporally sometime between 1977 and 1999. It's all very reminiscent of the opening of U2's 'Zooropa' album, which is no bad thing at all.

OUTSIDE

Those of you brave enough to have attended the first Tin Machine tour in 1989 might have heard a track called 'Now', which was featured on two of the UK dates. It forms the basis for 'Outside', which builds anthemically, courtesy of some rousing drumming from Sterling Campbell, into one of the album's best songs. Vocally, Bowie is understated and the lyric helps to herald in the new, fully-fledged post-modern Bowie, aching to blur past and present into a perpetual 'Now'. Theoretically he may be ten years out of date, but in pop, late is always better than never.

HEARTS FILTHY LESSON

I thought Bowie was bluffing when he said that he couldn't care less if nobody bought his records, but when this fine but overtly uncommercial track was promoted to lead-off single (when almost every other track on the album would have been a better choice), I concluded that either he was deliberately trying to sabotage the chances of his album doing well or genuinely couldn't chose a single for love nor money. 'Hearts Filthy Lesson' is an almost monotonal repetitive drone, ominous, frightening even, but a single it ain't... and the video, tremendous though it is, is so disturbing, even in its re-edited form (MTV refused to screen the original version), that it could never be considered for heavy rotation. Incidentally, the piano line sounds like a sample from Iggy and the Stooges' 'Raw Power' (1973).

A SMALL PLOT OF LAND

Who's been listening to Scott Walker's 'Tilt' then? Well, Bowie's almost operatic vocal on this track is a direct borrowing from the AWOL American and is set against some of Garson's most bonkers piano playing. A difficult listening experience, but at least it's better than almost anything on 'Tonight'.

SEGUE - BABY GRACE (A HORRID CASSETTE)

A short narrative with Bowie's vocal delivered in the guise of 14-year-old murder victim Baby Grace.

HALLO SPACEBOY

In terms of plot development this doesn't fit at all, but no matter. Although thematically it revisits the 'hi, I'm bi' Seventies persona, with its distorted thrash, catchy guitar riff which spins from speaker to speaker, and kitsch sci-fi synth refrain, it is another indication that Bowie really has moved musically into dangerous territory once again.

THE MOTEL

This track shows Bowie and Eno's minimalistic sensibilities interwoven to good effect with a wearied vocal performance set against Garson's languorous piano refrain.

I HAVE NOT BEEN TO OXFORD TOWN

There are definite echoes of 'Lodger''s 'Red Money' on this, the most catchy track on the album. This is Bowie at his very best in the persona of prime suspect Leon Blank, and the chorus and middle eight are top notch. And, as if you needed more, there's Alomar's clipped rhythm guitar to steal the show at the end.

NO CONTROL

This dark, sombre stab at Pet Shop Boys-styled techno works really well (they're a good group to borrow from), particularly since Bowie's on top form vocally, steering a delicate path between understatement and excess, as opposed to Neil Tennant's careful path between understatement and overstatement.

SEGUE – ALGERIA TOUCHSHRIEK

This is the silliest, and best, segue: Bowie is pushing eighty and yearning for another 'broken man' to rent his spare apartment.

THE VOYEUR OF UTTER DESTRUCTION (AS BEAUTY)

This time big, bad Dame David is none other than the Minotaur in another slice of 'Lodger'-era Bowie. As an aside, it was reported in the British press during 1995 that an anonymous man had offered Bowie and Damien Hirst his body (after death) for the sake of art, so that Hirst could graft on a bull's head and Bowie could reconstruct the Minotaur!

SEGUE – RAMONA A. STONE/I AM WITH NAME

Even if, for some, this may prove unlikeable, this segue is undoubtedly chilling and powerful in its execution. Which leads us on to...

WISHFUL BEGINNINGS

One of his most disturbing songs, with Bowie's vocal lilting like a blissful torturer about to pull the wings off a ladybird one by one.

WE PRICK YOU

Bowie described this dance track, with its infectious riff and screamed unison chorus, as 'dotty'. Its nearest soulmate in the Bowie oeuvre is perhaps the little-heard and even less admired 'Chilly Down' from the rightfully forgotten 'Labyrinth' soundtrack album.

SEGUE – NATHAN ADLER

After another spoken segue (Bowie now sounds like Frank Zappa's Central Scrutinizer from the Joe's Garage albums) we get...

I'M DERANGED

A fine dance track with echoes of late Kraftwerk in the backing track and distinct reminders of another, lesser, Bowie song, the Nile Rodgers-produced 'Real Cool World' (Warner WO127CD, 1992) in the melody.

THRU' THESE ARCHITECTS EYES

A storming, nay blistering cut, sung by Bowie as Leon Blank with one of those swooping melodies which he has been so adept at since the mid-Seventies. Musically one of the most conventional tracks on the album it prepares us neatly for...

SEGUE – NATHAN ADLER

A very short spoken section and then...

STRANGERS WHEN WE MEET

Another classic Bowie pop song, this time a re-working of a track from the criminally under-exposed *Buddha Of Suburbia*. Bowie and Eno really try to make this a 'son-of-'Heroes'' complete with a one-note sustained lead-guitar, instantly hooky bass guitar line and a beautiful melody which builds perfectly. An incongruous ending to an otherwise uncompromising album.

COMPILATIONS

EARLY MATERIAL

DAVID BOWIE: EARLY ON (1964-1966)

(US CD: RHINO R2 70526)

This 1991 compilation is an essential item for those interested in Bowie's musical beginnings. It collects together all there is from the period, including unreleased demos, and comes with Julie C. Stoller's informative liner notes.

Full track listing: 'Lisa Jane' (Davie Jones with The King Bees), 'Louie, Louie Go Home' (Davie Jones with The King Bees), 'I Pity The Fool' (The Manish Boys), 'Take My Tip' (The Manish Boys), 'That's Where My Heart Is' (previously unreleased demo), 'I Want My Baby Back' (previously unreleased demo), 'Bars Of The County Jail' (previously unreleased demo), 'You've Got A Habit Of Leaving' (Davy Jones), 'Baby Loves That Way' (Davy Jones), 'I'll Follow You' (previously unreleased Davy Jones track),

'Glad I've Got Nobody' (previously unreleased Davy Jones track), 'Can't Help Thinking About Me' (David Bowie with The Lower Third), 'And I Say To Myself' (David Bowie with The Lower Third), 'Do Anything You Say' (David Bowie), 'Good Morning Girl' (David Bowie), 'I Dig Everything' (David Bowie), 'I'm Not Losing Sleep' (David Bowie).

DAVID BOWIE: ROCK REFLECTIONS

(AUSTRALIAN CD: DERAM/POLYDOR 820 549 2 RELEASED 1990)

This Australian compilation is the old 'Images' compilation from the Seventies re-issued and it has been heavily imported. Other compilations of Deram material to consider are 'The David Bowie Collection'

(Castle CSCD 118), which contains all the tracks from his first Deram album plus 'The Laughing Gnome', The Gospel According To Tony Day', 'Did You Ever Have A Dream', 'The London Boys', 'Karma Man' and 'In The Heat Of The Morning', and the 1969 compilation 'The World Of David Bowie', with tracks chosen by ex-manager Ken Pitt, which was re-issued in Germany in 1992 (CD 844070 2).

Full track listing: 'Rubber Band', 'Maid Of Bond Street', 'Sell Me A Coat', 'Love You Till Tuesday', 'There Is A Happy Land', 'The Laughing Gnome', 'The Gospel According To Tony Day', 'Did You Ever Have A Dream', 'Uncle Arthur', 'We Are Hungry Men', 'When I Live My Dream', 'Join The Gang', 'Little Bombardier', 'Come And Buy My Toys', 'Silly Boy Blue', 'She's Got Medals', 'Please Mr Gravedigger', 'London Boys', 'Karma Man', 'Let Me Sleep Beside You', 'In The Heat Of The Morning'.

LOVE YOU TILL TUESDAY

(UK CD: PICKWICK PWKS 4131 P, RELEASED 13 MAY 1984;
UK CHART: 53 (TOTAL WEEKS IN CHART: 4)

A companion piece, plus additional tracks, to the video of the same name.

Tracks: 'Space Oddity', 'Love You Till Tuesday', 'When I'm 5', 'Ching-a-ling', 'The Laughing Gnome', 'Rubber Band', 'Sell Me A Coat', 'Liza Jane', 'When I Live My Dream', 'Let Me Sleep Beside You', 'The London Boy'.

LATER MATERIAL

SOUND + VISION

(US CD: RYKODISC RCD 90120/21/22; RELEASED NOVEMBER 1989)

Bowie's back catalogue has been the subject of seemingly endless repackaging with the result that, particularly in the 1980s, a lot of inferior material hit the record racks. In 1982 and 1983 RCA released all of Bowie's albums, excluding 'David Live' and 'Ziggy Stardust The Motion Picture', on CD, but supplies dried up when his licensing agreement with RCA expired in 1986. Bowie gave Rykodisc, a small Canadian label which had impressed him with their diligent and inventive repackaging of Frank Zappa's back catalogue, the opportunity to take on the not inconsiderable task of re-issuing all his records, with the exception of the narrated 'Peter And The Wolf' and the two greatest hits packages 'Changesone' and 'Changestwo', from 'Space Oddity' to 'Ziggy Stardust The Motion Picture'. Rykodisc did a pretty good job, although Bowiephiles were less than happy that tracks known to be in existence, such as two tracks demoed with John Cale ('Velvet Couch' and 'Pian -Ola' in 1979), were not included in the re-issue package as bonus tracks.

'Sound + Vision' was released just before the re-issuing schedule got under way and is still the best Bowie compilation ever. It is beautifully packaged and comprises three full-length CDs, a fourth containing three live tracks, and a CD video edit of 'Ashes To Ashes'.

Although officially a North American release only, it was heavily imported for a while into the UK and could be snapped up for around £50 on CD (a tenner more for its six-record vinyl counterpart). It was also available in a very limited 'wooden box' special edition containing a certificate of authenticity signed by Bowie himself. In November 1994 it was re-issued with a CD-ROM version of the 'Ashes To Ashes' video, and in October 1995 it was repackaged as 'Sound + Vision Revisited' as a normal-sized set of three CDs.

So what makes this compilation so special?

For a start, although there are a number of big hits thrown in, it concentrates on some of Bowie's best album tracks. Virtually all the other Bowie compilations stick to the hits, and this is only part of the story, as a good deal of his best work has never made it on to 7". So 'Big Brother' and 'Fascination' cuddle up with singles such as 'Ashes To Ashes' and 'John I'm Only Dancing'. Secondly, the set includes a number of rare Bowie tracks which were not subsequently part of Rykodisc's reissuing programme. These are:

SPACE ODDITY (DEMO)

An interesting demo featuring Bowie's friend 'Hutch'. Note Bowie's twee piece of self-promotion at the beginning when he addresses would-be sponsors.

LONDON BYE TA-TA

The track which was ear-marked by then manager Ken Pitt as the follow-up to 'Space Oddity' but was dropped in favour of 'The Prettiest Star'.

THE PRETTIEST STAR

The original single version with Marc Bolan on lead guitar.

JOHN I'M ONLY DANCING

Gutsy, 'Aladdin Sane' out-take with saxophone high in the mix and superior to the 1972 single version. This version also found its way on to some copies of 'ChangesOne Bowie' (now deleted).

1984/DODO (MEDLEY)

An early, less disco-inflected version of '1984' coupled with a version of 'Dodo' which is different from the one used by Rykodisc when they reissued the Diamond Dogs album.

REBEL REBEL (RARE US SINGLE VERSION)

A good, echo-laden edit with Bowie apparently playing all instruments. It was this version, not the more well-known British version, which became the blueprint for the song's live renditions.

AFTER TODAY

This out-take from 'Young Americans' is a solid if unspectacular track.

IT'S HARD TO BE A SAINT IN THE CITY

This frenetic cover of the Springsteen song is

from the 'Station To Station' sessions. An earlier version is said to be in the Mainman vaults and possibly dates from the Young Americans period.

HELDEN (1989 REMIX)

'Heroes' sung well in German and given a dusting-down by Bowie.

Also included are three live tracks recorded in Boston at The Music Hall, 1 October,1972: 'John I'm Only Dancing', 'Changes' and 'The Superman', together with a CD video version of the classic Bowie video of 'Ashes To Ashes'.

CHANGESBOWIE

(UK CD: EMI BD TV 1, RELEASED 12 MARCH 1990; US CD: RYKODISC RCD 20171 UK CHART: 1 [TOTAL WEEKS IN CHART 29] US CHART: 39)

EMI's decision to re-issue what was essentially the 1976 compilation ChangesOneBowie (UK Number 2, US Number 10) with the addition of eight subsequent hits already widely available smacked of RCA-scale fleecing. Even the cover was a horrendously boring re-run of

that album's monochrome cover shot, with a few even more boring colour photos added for good measure. Only the addition of a 1990 re-mix of 'Fame' could possibly have tempted Bowie fans to buy what they already had, and since this very soon became available as a single in its own right (EMI USA FAME 90), there was little point.

Released to capitalise on Bowie's Sound + Vision tour this is an unimaginative collection of Bowie crowd-pleasers. They're all fine tracks to be sure, but this collection has since been superseded by the preferable double CD 'The Singles Collection'. Perhaps most aggravating of all, in a move which beggared belief, the vinyl and cassette version of the album contained three bonus tracks left off the CD version – 'Starman', 'Life On Mars?' and 'Sound and Vision'.

Full track listing: 'Space Oddity', 'John I'm Only Dancing', 'Changes', 'Ziggy Stardust', 'Suffragette City', 'Jean Genie', 'Diamond Dogs', 'Rebel Rebel', 'Young Americans', 'Fame '90' (remix), 'Golden Years', 'Heroes', 'Ashes To Ashes', 'Fashion', 'Let's Dance', 'China Girl', 'Modern Love', 'Blue Jean'.

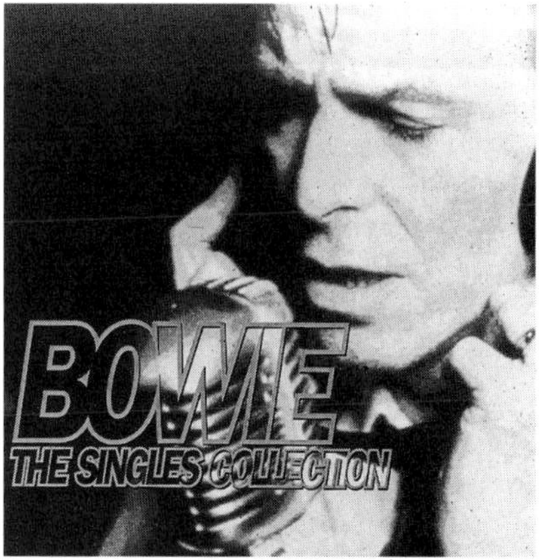

BOWIE: THE SINGLES COLLECTION

(UK CD: EMI 7243 8 28099 2 0, US CD: RYKODISC RCD 10218/9; RELEASED 8 NOVEMBER 1993; UK CHART: 9)

For those of you coming new to Bowie then this is probably the place to start, although again the focus is on the big hits – though nobody seems quite sure about what songs were actually singles ('Ziggy Stardust', for example, was never an A-side anywhere in the world). There are two simi-

lar versions of this compilation, and the Rykodisc edition available in North America shades the EMI version by taking the story up to the Nineties with 'Jump They Say' and through a slightly better track selection. This Rykodisc edition omitted five tracks: 'Rock'n'Roll Suicide', 'Knock On Wood', 'Alabama Song', 'Wild Is The Wind' and 'This Is Not America', but added eight: 'Oh You Pretty Things!', 'Be My Wife', 'Look Back In Anger', 'Cat People (Puttin' Out Fire)', 'Loving The Alien' (single version), 'Never Let Me Down' and 'Jump They Say' (single version). The Rykodisc edition also contained a limited edition CD of Bowie's 1977 duet with Bing Crosby, 'Little Drummer Boy/Peace On Earth'

The full track listing for the EMI version is as follows, Disc 1: 'Space Oddity', 'Changes', 'Starman', 'Ziggy Stardust', 'Suffragette City', 'John I'm Only Dancing', 'The Jean Genie', 'Drive In Saturday', 'Life On Mars?', 'Sorrow', 'Rebel Rebel', 'Rock'n'Roll Suicide', 'Diamond Dogs', 'Knock On Wood', 'Young Americans', 'Fame', 'Golden Years', 'TVC 15', 'Sound And Vision'; Disc 2: 'Heroes', 'Beauty And The Beast', 'Boys Keep Swinging', 'DJ', 'Alabama Song', 'Ashes To Ashes', 'Fashion', 'Scary Monsters (And Super Creeps)', 'Under Pressure', 'Wild Is The Wind', 'Let's Dance', 'China Girl', 'Modern Love', 'Blue Jean', 'This Is Not America', 'Dancing In The Streets', 'Absolute Beginners', 'Day-in Day-out'.

The following tracks have not previously been dealt with in detail in the analysis:

CAT PEOPLE (PUTTING OUT FIRE)

[RYKODISC VERSION ONLY]

This is the full twelve-inch single version from the *Cat People* soundtrack, not the revamped version to be found on 'Let's Dance'. This is the preferred version, with Bowie's vocal coolly set off by disco guru Giorgio Moroder's instantly recognisable production.

DANCING IN THE STREET

Without wishing to deny its significance in terms of consciousness-raising, musically, Live Aid wasn't anything special. It did, however. present Jagger and Bowie with the excuse to record this rather irritating cover version of the Martha Reeves and The Vandellas standard and make a light-hearted video together. A UK Number 1 naturally.

LITTLE DRUMMER BOY/ PEACE ON EARTH

[BONUS CD ON RYKODISC VERSION]

This duet with Bing Crosby, recorded shortly before Crosby's death in 1977, is one of the most surreal moments in pop history: the thirty-year-old former androgyny teaming up with the bumbling cardigan Bing, forty-four years his senior. Despite repeated claims to the contrary by po-faced journalists, this is a stirring schmaltzy Yuletide epic and the two crooners are a swell gel.

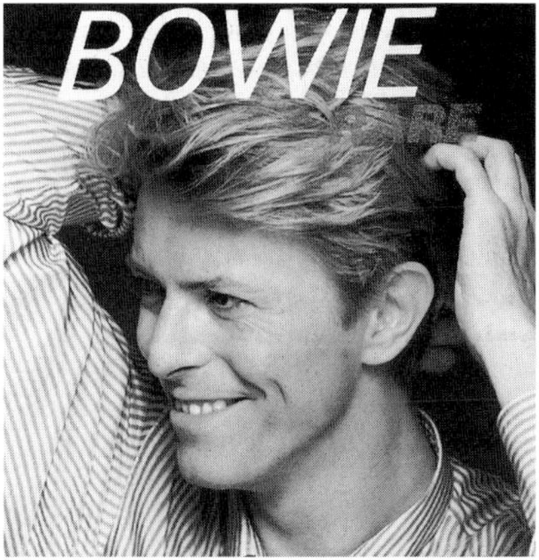

RARESTONE BOWIE

(UK CD: TRIDENT INTERNATIONAL GOLDEN YEARS GY 002, RELEASED 19 JUNE 1995)

Another in the series of MainMan/ Trident International re-issues. Containing eight live tracks and Bowie's studio version of 'All The Young Dudes' it's a little over 36 minutes long and so hardly tempts with value-for-money. That said, hard-core Bowie fans will definitely want to have it.

ALL THE YOUNG DUDES

Bowie's 'original' studio version dates from the 'Aladdin Sane' sessions and thus post-dates Mott The Hoople's hit version by over six months. It's a strangely muted affair with Bowie's jazzy sax to the fore and the chorus rather thrown away.

QUEEN BITCH

A live, funked-up version recorded at Long Island, New York on 23 March, 1976.

SOUND AND VISION

Although then a recent hit single, Bowie only gave this Bowie-favourite one airing on the 1978 Stage tour, at Earl's Court on 1 July – and here it is.

TIME

A live version from the 1980 Floor Show recorded in October 1973.

BE MY WIFE

Another flashback to the 1978 tour, and again from Earl's Court, July 1. Since neither 'Be My Wife' nor 'Sound And Vision' made it on to the largely disappointing official live album of the tour, 'Stage', these two tracks are worth a listen.

FOOTSTOMPIN'/ WISH I COULD SHIMMY LIKE MY SISTER KATE

This is from the *Dick Cavett Show* broadcast in the US on 4 December, 1974.

ZIGGY STARDUST

Live cut from Santa Monica in October 1972.

MY DEATH

Interesting version of the Jacques Brel standard, despite Bowie's warning to the audience that his voice was shot, and taken from the Ziggy show at the Carnegie Hall, New York City, 28 September, 1972.

I FEEL FREE

Very early version of The Cream's 'I Feel Free' from a Ziggy gig at the Kingston Polytechnic, UK, on 6 May, 1972. Warning: this would be bog-standard quality even for a bootleg.

SOUNDTRACK RECORDINGS

ABSOLUTE BEGINNERS

(ORIGINAL UK ISSUE: VIRGIN V 2386, RELEASED MARCH 1986; UK CD: VIRGIN CDV 2386 UK CHART: 19 [TOTAL WEEKS IN CHART: 9])

Contains three Bowie tracks: 'Absolute Beginners', 'That's Motivation' and 'Volare'.

LABYRINTH

(ORIGINAL UK ISSUE: EMI AMERICA AML 3104, RELEASED JUNE 1986; UK CD: EMI AMERICA CDP 746312 2; UK CHART: 38 [TOTAL WEEKS IN CHART: 2])

Soundtrack to the Jim Henson fantasy film. It contains a score by Trevor Jones and six undemanding Bowie tracks co-produced by Arif Mardin. The gospel-influenced sing-a-long 'Underground' (which certainly influenced Madonna and her 'Like A Prayer' single three years later) was a UK Number 21 hit. Tracks are 'Underground (opening titles)', 'Magic Dance', 'Chilly Down', 'As The World Falls Down', 'Within You', 'Underground'.

MISCELLANEOUS

PETER AND THE WOLF

(ORIGINAL UK ISSUE: RCA RL 12743, RELEASED MAY 1978; UK CD: RCA RD 82743)

Bowie narrates *Peter And The Wolf* before Eugene Ormandy conducts the Philadelphia Orchestra through Britten's 'Young Person's Guide To The Orchestra'. The cover photo, lifted from the 'ChangesoneBowie' sessions and showing an austere and unsmiling Thin White Duke, must have spooked both parent and child, thus accounting for the album's poor sales.

It was re-issued on CD in the States by BMG Classics/ RCA Victor (GD 60878) in 1992 with a new cover and Tchaikovsky's *Nutcracker Suite* tacked on.

VIDEOS

Up until the release of 'Bowie: The Video Collection' in 1993, Bowie fans were incredibly short-changed when it came to seeing their man on video. This was indeed a crazy situation given Bowie's photogenic stage shows and videos, and even now there are many gaps to be filled. There is no footage available on video from any of his Seventies concerts, bar the Ziggy farewell gig, or from the visually innovative Sound + Vision 1990 tour. Bowie's many excellent appearances on television, and the best documentary on Bowie ever – Omnibus' *Cracked Actor*, originally screened in 1975 – are all unavailable on home video.

In this section I've concentrated on currently available product, giving the latest release date wherever possible (many of the Bowie videos have been repackaged and re-released three time over). I have excluded Bowie's films.

LOVE YOU TILL TUESDAY

(VIDEO: POLYGRAM SUPC 00022, LASER DISC: IMAGE ENTERTAINMENT 6307)

Bowie made this film consisting of eight proto-pop promos, including the original studio version of 'Space Oddity' and a mime called *The Mask*, in 1969. It runs for 28 minutes.

ZIGGY STARDUST AND THE SPIDERS FROM MARS

(WARNER PES 38022)

This is the video of the D.A. Pennebaker film of the famous Ziggy retirement gig at the Hammersmith Odeon on July 3, 1973. Its rather grainy texture does not do justice to the serene Kabuki-styled Bowie or Mick Ronson's trousers, but there's still plenty of fun, including Bowie doing his Marcel Marceau act on 'A Width Of A Circle'. On the subject of trousers, two tracks performed that night – 'Jean Genie/Love Me Do' and 'Round And Round' (which featured guitarist Jeff Beck) are annoyingly not included. It is rumoured that Beck was subsequently appalled by the appearance of his flares and gave this as a reason (a very stupid one) for pulling the plug. This doesn't account for the non-appearance of the tracks on the 1992 CD release (unless, of course, the flares squeaked mid-solo).

SERIOUS MOONLIGHT

(WARNER MUSIC VISION 4509 968 393)

Originally released in two instalments, this complete version is the one to go for and is a fine video keepsake of Bowie's biggest tour to date. With hindsight it's all a bit too slick and staid, but Bowie's hair, backcombed and lacquered into a frenzy, is still worth a giggle. Highlights include a resurrected 'Cracked Actor', complete with skull and cloak as props, and an extended version of 'Fame'. Mysteriously, the tour's usual closing number, 'Modern Love', is nowhere to be found.

RICOCHET

(VIRGIN VVD 084)

Also from the Serious Moonlight tour, this video contains some concert footage with some staged, though interesting, shots of Bowie going about his daily business in the Far East (in hotel rooms, on escalators, in a taxi, visiting a Buddhist shrine). There's also a distracting and weak story line intercut with material about a young fan trying to raise the dosh for a Bowie ticket. Inessential, unless, once again, you've got the 'Bowies' bad.

JAZZIN' FOR BLUE JEAN

(VIDEO: VIDEO COLLECTION PM 0017, LASER DISC: PIONEER ARTISTS VIDEO 113)

This is a twenty-minute, Julien Temple-directed extended pop promo dating from 1984. The video tells the story of Vic (played by Bowie), a cockney nerd, and his attempt to win over his love by taking her to a concert by Screaming Lord Byron, Vic's outlandish *doppelganger* (also played by Bowie). A piss-take of the preciousness of pop megalomania in general, and Bowie's in particular, the video itself is well worth looking out for.

GLASS SPIDER

(VIDEO: MUSIC CLUB, LASER DISC: IMAGE ENTERTAINMENT 6198)

Like Serious Moonlight this originally came in two instalments, but get the edited-together version issued in 1990 if you can as it is better value for money. The Glass Spider tour was mauled at the time and it is plain to see that Bowie had over-stretched himself (probably literally!), abseiling from the top of sixty-foot spiders one minute, strangled by ropes the next. The theatricality isn't arty and it isn't camp, falling somewhere in that showbiz grey area inhabited by lesser lights such as Prince and Michael Jackson. But there are such delights as 'Absolute Beginners' and 'Time' along the way. The Sound + Vision tour of 1990 did it all much better, but remains undocumented on video.

TIN MACHINE LIVE – OY VEY, BABY

(POLYGRAM 085 320 3)

On which we get almost an hour and a half of Tin Machine (seventeen songs in all) filmed by Rudi Dolezal and Hannes Rossacher (aka 'The Torpedo Twins') at The Docks, Hamburg on the 24 October, 1991. They do a grand job but they're fighting a losing battle. Tin Machine live were often the ultimate rock-and-roll cliché. Boring guitar solos, a semi-naked tattooed tub-thumping drummer, and three iffy cover versions including the very dodgy 'Go Now', the oldie from The Moody Blues which they did considerably better. It's all such a shame since some of the material deserved better than this flailing, and The Sales Brothers, who were fine with Iggy Pop in the Seventies, are now too forced with their rock camaraderie-by-numbers act. By this time everyone must have been getting up each others' noses – as opposed to the Seventies, when they were putting everything up each others' noses.

BLACK TIE WHITE NOISE

(BMG VIDEO 74321 16622 3)

In order to try and make amends for the decision not to tour in 1993 Bowie decided to release this, a video companion piece for the 'Black Tie White Noise' album, consisting of an interview, six 'live' tracks recorded that May in the Hollywood Center Studios in LA, and the three video clips for 'Miracle Goodnight', 'Jump They Say' and 'Black Tie White Noise'. The interview material is mildly interesting but the 'live' tracks, in actuality mimed performances directed by David Mallet, are mostly plain boring and look incredibly cheaply done. Bowie redeems himself however with two of his very best promo clips. 'Miracle Goodnight' is a carousel of harlequinesque images and 'Jump They Say', with its Hitchcockean undercurrents, rivals 'Ashes To Ashes' for sheer power and invention. If you haven't seen these two, 'Black Tie White Noise' is an essential purchase.

BOWIE: THE VIDEO COLLECTION

(PMI PM 807)

Bowie's legendary power as a pop icon was based as much on the way he looked and the way he packaged himself as on the music itself, and this video, containing twenty-five videos and covering the period 1972-1990, provides the vision as well as the sound. Again there are some grouses. Where, for example, are Bowie's television appearances for 'Rebel Rebel', 'Young Americans', 'Fame' and 'Golden Years', which have long since masqueraded as promos for the singles? And what happened to the clip for 'The Drowned Girl' from the 'Baal EP' in 1982?

But this is perhaps churlish bearing in mind the brilliance contained herein. The earliest promos such as 'Space Oddity' and 'Jean Genie' don't really do the startling Ziggy justice but by 1973 and 'Life On Mars?' the stark white backdrop frames the carrot-topped rocker perfectly. Then there's an unnecessarily big leap forward to the late Seventies and to an exquisitely weird Bowie performing 'Be My Wife'. After then the videos get slicker and more multi-layered as Bowie begins to move away from simple performance videos (with the exception of the only real disappointment, 'Modern Love') in order to take on bigger themes such as colonial politics on 'Let's Dance' and urban American low-life on 'Day In-Day Out'. 'Ashes To Ashes' is still a stunning clip, filmed in part on location at Beachy Head, and featuring Bowie as astronaut, asylum inmate and Pierrot respectively. However, the famous drag video for 'Boys Keep Swinging' is more radical and 'Fashion', 'DJ' and 'Look Back In Anger' just as cool. During the Eighties Bowie's videos declined in their power to shock and provoke but still kept up a consistently good standard, particularly on the Antipodean 'Let's Dance' and the sombre, moody, little-seen black-and-white clip for 'Wild Is The Wind'. As an added incentive to buy (as if one is needed), the video for the planned, but never released, single from the Labyrinth album, 'As The World Falls Down', is also to be found along side the hammy but good 'Loving The Alien' and the studied nostalgia of 'Absolute Beginners'. And finally we get 'Fame '90', one of the best of the lot, with Bowie and Canadian dancer Louise LeCavalier artily framed by a wall of television sets showing re-runs of Bowie's past visual selves. Absolutely essential stuff and, as *Q*'s Dave Cavanagh concluded, 'the greatest video collection ever seen'.

The full track listing is as follows: 'Space Oddity' (1972), 'John I'm Only Dancing' (1972), 'The Jean Genie' (1972), 'Life On Mars?' (1973), 'Be My Wife' (1977), 'Heroes' (1979), 'Boys Keep Swinging' (1979), 'Look Back In Anger' (1979), 'DJ' (1979), 'Ashes To Ashes' (1980), 'Fashion' (1980), 'Wild Is The Wind' (1982), 'Let's Dance' (1983), 'China Girl' (1983), 'Modern Love' (1983), 'Blue Jean' (1984), 'Loving The Alien' (1985), 'Dancing In The Street' (1985), 'Absolute Beginners' (1986), 'Underground' (1986), 'As The World Falls Down' (1986), 'Day In Day Out' (1987), 'Time Will Crawl' (1987), 'Never Let Me Down' (1987), 'Fame '90' (1990).

You can also find other non-essential Bowie performances, short interviews and cameos on a variety of other videos. For example, for those who want to relive one of his worst moments, Bowie crops up duetting with Tina Turner on two songs on her 1985 'Private Dancer Plays Live' video (PMI MVP 99 1085 2). He can also be found introducing Raymond Briggs' genuinely great short animated film *The Snowman* (Palace PVC 3090 A), complete with tight-fitting jumper and peroxide blond hair.

INTERACTIVE MEDIA

It came as no surprise that the audiovisually talented Bowie would be one of the first to branch out into the world of interactivity. At the time of writing just one Bowie CD-ROM is in existence, made to accompany the 'Black Tie White Noise' album and called 'Jump'. It allows you to mix your own music for the 'Black Tie White Noise' track and to re-invent the video for 'Jump They Say'. The 'Outside' CD-ROM was released in 1996.

INDEX